W9-ARK-210

★ ★ ★ ★ ★ ★ ★ ★ ★ ★

Harry S Truman, President

OTHER BOOKS IN THE PRESIDENTIAL BIOGRAPHY SERIES

★ ★ ★ ★ ★ ★ ★ ★ ★ ★ ★ ★ ★ ★ ★ ★

Harry S Truman, President

Thomas Fleming

WALKER AND COMPANY
NEW YORK

First published in the United States of America in 1993
by Walker Publishing Company, Inc.

Published simultaneously in Canada by Thomas Allen & Son
Canada, Limited, Markham, Ontario

Library of Congress Cataloging-in-Publication Data
Fleming, Thomas J.
Harry S Truman, president / by Thomas Fleming.
p.; cm. — (Presidential biography series)
Includes bibliographical references (p.) and index.
Summary: A biography of the thirty-third president of the United
States.
ISBN 0-8027-8267-1. — ISBN 0-8027-8269-8 (lib. bdg.)
1. Truman, Harry S, 1884–1972 — Juvenile literature.   2. United
States — Politics and government — 1945–1953 — Juvenile literature.
3. Presidents — United States — Biography — Juvenile literature.
[1. Truman, Harry S, 1884–1972.   2. Presidents.]   I. Title.
II. Series.
E814.F57   1993
973.918'092 — dc20   93 — 153
[B]   CIP
AC

Printed in the United States of America

2   4   6   8   10   9   7   5   3   1

Book design by Shelli Rosen

Contents

* * * * * * * * * * *

Harry S Truman,
President

Harry, the President Is Dead

At 5:00 on the afternoon of April 12, 1945, Vice President Harry S Truman strolled into the office of Sam Rayburn, Speaker of the House of Representatives and an old friend. They planned to spend an hour discussing legislation and the world situation. American, British, and Russian armies were smashing into the heart of Nazi Germany. The American navy and marines and army were fighting a ferocious battle with the Japanese in the Pacific for the island of Okinawa. After almost four years of global violence, World War II was roaring to a climax.

"Harry," Sam Rayburn said in his Texas drawl, "Steve Early wants you to call the White House."

Early was President Franklin D. Roosevelt's press secretary. Truman put through the call. "Please come right over as quickly and as quietly as you can," Early said in a strained voice.

By 5:25, thanks to some fast driving by Tom Harty, Truman's government chauffeur, the vice president was at 1600 Pennsylvania Avenue. For the previous two weeks, President Roosevelt had been at Warm Springs, Georgia, where he seemed to be recuperating from the extreme exhaustion that had made many people, including the vice president, worry about his health. Truman told himself FDR had returned to Washington unexpectedly, and wanted to see him about some of the problems the administration was having getting bills through Congress.

Inside the White House, the vice president was immediately escorted upstairs to Eleanor Roosevelt's second-floor study. The president's wife was with Steve Early and her daughter, Anna Roosevelt Boettiger. Gently, with great dignity, she put her arm around Truman's shoulder. "Harry," she said. "The president is dead."

For a moment Truman could neither think nor speak. Typically, his first thought was of Mrs. Roosevelt's grief and pain. "Is there anything I can do for you?" he said.

"Is there anything we can do for *you?*" she said with a grave smile. "You're the one in trouble now."

Harry Truman realized she was right. He had just become president of the most powerful nation in the world, in the middle of a global war. Never before in American history had a president faced such a staggering array of problems and decisions.

In his quiet way, Harry Truman took charge. He ordered a car sent to his Connecticut Avenue apartment for his wife, Bess, and his daughter, Margaret. He telephoned them and told them the terrible news. The secretary of state, Edward Stettinius, arrived, tears streaming down his cheeks. He urged Truman to call a cabinet meeting immediately. Truman agreed—and nine cabinet members soon hurried to the White House.

Truman asked the attorney general, Francis Biddle, to call the chief justice of the Supreme Court, Harlan Fiske Stone, and ask him to come to the White House and administer the oath of office. Meanwhile, Steve Early and his staff were ransacking the building for a Bible.

In an hour, Mrs. Truman, Margaret, the nine cabinet members, several White House staffers, and a half dozen congressional leaders gathered in the cabinet room. The staffers had finally located a small red-edged Bible. Truman stood at the head of a long table, beneath a portrait of Woodrow Wilson, who happened to be his favorite president. He held the Bible in his left hand, raised his right hand, and repeated after the chief justice the oath as it is written in the Constitution.

"I, Harry S Truman, do solemnly swear that I will faithfully execute the office of president of the United States, and will to the best of my ability protect and defend the Constitution of the United States."

Harry S Truman is sworn in as president after the death of Franklin D. Roosevelt on April 12, 1945. Beneath his thumb in the hand that is holding the Bible, Truman had a small piece of paper on which the presidential oath was typed. He gave it to his daughter, Margaret, as a souvenir. (NATIONAL PARK SERVICE, ABBIE ROWE, COURTESY HARRY S TRUMAN LIBRARY)

"So help you God," said the chief justice, revealing his own deep emotion. Though the words were not part of the official oath, George Washington had said them when he was inaugurated in 1789.

"So help me God," Truman said, and raised the Bible to his lips.

Behind him, the clock on the mantelpiece read 7:09. One hundred and four minutes before, Harry Truman had arrived at the White House expecting to see the president of the United States. Now he was president.

Captain Harry Goes to Washington

Harry Truman was born on May 10, 1884, on his family's six-hundred-acre farm in Grandview, Missouri, about eighteen miles from Kansas City. His father, John Truman, ran the farm in partnership with his father-in-law, Solomon Young. Harry's mother and father could not agree on his middle name. They decided to let it stand as S, which honored both Solomon Young and Mr. Truman's father, whose middle name was Shippe.

Among Harry's earliest memories is a game he played with his younger brother, Vivian, and a neighbor's boy. "We discovered a mud hole at the end of a maple grove and I pulled my wagon with the boys into it and upset it. We repeated it several times, taking turns landing in the mud. When my mother found us, we were plastered with mud and water from head to foot. What a grand spanking I got as the ringleader!"

Vivian was three years younger than Harry. Two years after his birth, the two boys acquired a baby sister, Mary Jane. From the start, Harry and Vivian regarded their sister as a very special person, whom they were determined

Harry S Truman (right) at the age of four with his brother, Vivian (left), two years old. (HARRY S TRUMAN LIBRARY)

to protect and cherish. Harry was especially fond of her. He often braided her hair and sang her to sleep at night.

All three children were deeply devoted to their mother, who was by far the strongest personality in the family. Martha Ellen Young had graduated from the Baptist Female College in Lexington, Missouri, where she had majored in music and art. She was determined to give her children a good education.

With his mother's help, Harry learned to read by the time he was five years old. But his mother noticed he had to squint to read a newspaper. She took him to an eye doctor, who fitted him with thick glasses and warned him against playing sports where he might break them.

That meant Harry spent a lot of time reading. By the time he had graduated from grammar school, he had read all the books in the Independence Public Library and had gone through the family Bible three times. His favorite subject was history. It was far more than romantic adventure to him. "It was solid instruction and wise teaching which I somehow felt I wanted and needed," he said later.

While he was still a boy, Harry realized history had some extremely valuable lessons to teach. Looking back fifty years later, he wrote: "I learned from it that a leader was a man who has the ability to get other people to do what they don't want to do, and like it. I learned that in those periods of history where there was no leadership, society usually groped through dark ages. My debt to history cannot be calculated. I know of no other motivation which accounts for my interest in the principles of leadership and government."

Young Harry Truman did not spend all his time thinking about history. In 1892, a very important person entered his life. His family had moved to Independence, Mis-

Harry Truman at age fifteen. By this time he had read all the books in the Independence Public Library. He was also a very good pianist and a fiendish practical joker. (HARRY S TRUMAN LIBRARY)

souri, a few miles closer to Kansas City, because the schools were better than the ones in Grandview. Young Harry's father went into business as a horse-and-mule trader. In Sunday school Harry met a beautiful blond girl named Bess Wallace.

They went to different grammar schools for a while, but they met again in the fifth grade. Later he admitted it took him months to get up the nerve to speak to her. "She sat behind me in the sixth, seventh, and high school grades," he said. "I thought she was the most beautiful person on earth."

A Truman cousin says: "There never was but one girl in the world for Harry Truman."

Along with being pretty, Bess Wallace was a remarkable athlete. She played third base on the local sandlot team and was the best tennis player in Independence. She also fenced very well, was a demon ice skater, an excellent horseback rider—and once won a shot-put prize in a track meet. Why did Harry Truman, whose athletic ability was zero, think he could attract such a young woman? Within this quiet young man with the thick glasses, there was a lot of self-confidence.

Although Harry got very good marks, he was not the best student in the class. That honor belonged to Charlie Ross, a lean, shy young man who had another talent Harry did not possess: he was a very good writer. Charlie was the editor of the yearbook and the class valedictorian— the one who gave a speech to parents and friends at the graduation ceremony. Their teacher, Miss Tillie Brown, liked the speech so much, she gave Charlie a big kiss. Harry Truman and several other boys protested this favoritism. "When you do something worthwhile, you'll get your reward too," Miss Tillie said.

Harry never forgot those words.

In his last year in high school, Harry decided he wanted to do more than read about history—he wanted to make it. He applied for the U.S. Military Academy at West Point. He easily passed the entrance examinations, but his bad eyes stopped him. Worse, his father ran into financial difficulties and could not send Harry to college.

He went back to reading history and worked as a bank clerk for a while. Then his father asked him to help run the family farm in Grandview. His grandfather, Solomon Young, had died, and his father's health was not good. From 1906 to 1917, Harry plowed and harvested those 600 acres. It was hard work and often it was discouraging because the money he got for his corn and wheat depended on the market price, which varied from year to year. Almost every weekend, he took a train to Independence to visit Bess Wallace.

Then history exploded, blowing Harry Truman and a lot of other people out of their hometowns. In Europe, the Germans and the empire of Austria-Hungary began fighting the British, the French, and the Russians. Soon millions of men were bleeding and dying on the western and eastern fronts in World War I. German submarines began sinking American ships carrying food and guns and ammunition to the Allies. When the Germans ignored President Woodrow Wilson's warnings, he went before Congress on April 2, 1917, and asked for a declaration of war.

When Harry Truman failed to get into West Point, he did the next best thing for a man who was interested in military affairs—he joined the National Guard. These amateur soldiers met for several weeks each summer to train with the latest weapons. When war was declared, Congress drafted the National Guard into the U.S. Army and Harry Truman became captain of Battery D of the 129th Field Artillery in the 35th Division.

The year is 1917 and First Lieutenant Harry S Truman has just taken command of the wild Irishmen of Battery D, 129th Field Artillery. He was soon promoted to captain. (HARRY S TRUMAN LIBRARY)

Battery D was composed of unruly Irish-Americans from Kansas City. They had already forced two captains to resign and looked forward to finishing off this fellow with thick glasses even faster. They soon learned what a lot of other people discovered in years to come: No one pushed Harry Truman around. In a very short time, Battery D was the best disciplined, most efficient outfit in the 35th Division.

In France, Battery D went into action on September 6, 1918, firing 3,000 rounds in four hours. Captain Truman

In July 1918, Captain Truman rides his horse through Camp Coetquidan, in Brittany, France, where the 129th Field Artillery trained before going into action against the Germans. Truman took three pairs of eyeglasses with him to France. Without his glasses he was almost blind. (HARRY S TRUMAN LIBRARY)

frequently risked his life to operate as a forward observer, reporting back on where the shells were falling so they could correct the ranges. In October, during the battle of the Argonne, the Germans counterattacked the 35th Division and came close to routing it. Only deadly fire from Captain Truman's guns and the other batteries of the 129th Field Artillery stopped them.

In 1919, Harry Truman came home with a confident stride. He had proven he could lead men and fight the German army to a standstill. His first order of business was to marry Bess Wallace. Knowing he was one of the most popular officers in the division, a fellow veteran, Eddie Jacobson, suggested that they go into business together running a clothing store. In those days it was called a haberdashery.

For a while the store flourished. Both men worked hard, twelve hours a day, six days a week. But in 1920, the country slid into a recession. The price of wheat dropped sharply and very few people in Kansas City had the money to buy clothes. By 1922, Truman and Jacobson had closed their doors. A proud man, Harry Truman never filed for bankruptcy. He paid off all his creditors, a few dollars at a time, over the next ten years.

Another 35th Division veteran, Mike Pendergast, had known and liked Truman in the army. He urged him to run for county judge. Mike's brother, Tom Pendergast, was the boss of the Kansas City Democratic political machine. Many cities were run by bosses like Tom, who put up candidates, got out the vote, and controlled the business side of running the city and county. With Mike's urging, Tom backed Truman. Army veterans liked the idea of voting for "Captain Harry." Truman won in a landslide.

A judge in Jackson County, Missouri, did not preside at criminal trials. He and two other judges were the ad-

Thirty-four-year-old Harry S Truman, just home from France, married his childhood sweetheart, thirty-three-year-old Bess Wallace. Here they pose in the garden of her home on North Delaware Street in Independence. He carried her picture in the pocket of his tunic throughout the war. (HARRY S TRUMAN LIBRARY)

"Captain Harry" poses with friends in his haberdashery at 104 West 12th Street in Kansas City. Although Truman and his partner, Eddie Jacobson, worked twelve hours a day, the store failed in the recession of 1921, leaving Truman $12,000 in debt. (HARRY S TRUMAN LIBRARY)

ministrators of the county. Truman did a good job for two years. He helped reduce the county's debt by $600,000. But when he ran for reelection, he collided with the Ku Klux Klan. Founded after the Civil War to maintain white control in the South, the Klan had expanded into border states like Missouri after World War I. It preached hatred of blacks, Jews, and Catholics.

Harry Truman refused to have anything to do with the Klan. They campaigned against him with vicious, slanderous statements. Helped by a split within the Democratic party, they beat him for reelection in 1924 — the only campaign he ever lost. At almost the same time, his daughter Margaret was born. Struggling to earn a living, Truman worked for the Automobile Club of Kansas City, launched a savings and loan association, and became head of a travel club. But his heart was still in politics, and Tom Pendergast still thought he made a good candidate. In 1926, with the boss's backing, he ran for chief judge of Jackson County and won.

For the next eight years, Truman ran Jackson County with a sure hand. In a political atmosphere famous for corruption, he was scrupulously honest. He was also intelligent. He saw that Jackson County desperately needed good roads if it was to cope with the constantly growing number of automobiles. With little help from a reluctant Tom Pendergast, who feared a bad political defeat, Truman persuaded the voters to approve bond issues for $7 million in new roads. Most of them are still in use today. He also built a magnificent new courthouse. Outside it he put up a superb statue of another favorite president, Andrew Jackson, on horseback.

A lot of contractors, eager to build the roads, thought they could use Tom Pendergast's influence to get the business. They, too, found out Harry Truman was hard to push around. At one point, twelve contractors persuaded Tom to meet with them and Truman, hoping to scare him. Truman did not budge. He said no one would get any work from him unless they made the lowest bid for the project—and guaranteed the quality of the materials they used. "I told you he was the hardheadedest, orneriest man in the world," Pendergast said. "There isn't anything I can do."

Truman's reputation for honesty and efficiency soon spread beyond the borders of Jackson County. People urged him to run for governor in 1932. But he insisted on staying for his second full term as presiding judge. In 1934, boss Tom Pendergast found himself badly in need of a candidate for the U.S. Senate. The St. Louis Democratic machine was pushing its own man. Tom decided Harry Truman was his man.

Even *The Kansas City Star,* which regularly opposed Pendergast candidates, admitted Truman was a man of "unimpeachable character and integrity." They reluctantly conceded that he was the best candidate, and the voters agreed, especially the farmers in hundreds of Missouri's small towns that Truman visited in his vigorous campaign. On January 3, 1935, Harry Truman took his seat as the junior senator from Missouri.

As a student of history, he was awed to find himself where Daniel Webster, Henry Clay, John C. Calhoun, and other famous senators had once orated. Many of the current crop of senators were almost as famous. Their names were in the newspapers every day.

Then an older senator slapped him on the back. "Don't let them scare you, Harry," he said. "For the first six months you'll wonder how you got here. After that you'll wonder how the rest of us got here."

Senator Harry S Truman of Missouri strides down the steps of the Capitol in Washington, D.C. Elected in 1934, Truman became known as one of the hardest workers in the Senate. During World War II his Truman Committee investigated defense industries and saved taxpayers billions of dollars. (COPYRIGHT UNKNOWN)

3

From Outsider to Insider

For his first few years in the Senate, Harry Truman worked hard and said little. He realized he was not a great orator. He also saw that the Senate was divided into grandstanders and workers. The grandstanders made lots of speeches and got plenty of headlines. But they were seldom respected by their fellow senators because they were never around to do the hard work of writing and passing laws.

The United States was in the grip of the Great Depression. Banks and corporations had collapsed. Millions of Americans were jobless. In the White House, Franklin D. Roosevelt, the first Democratic president in twelve years, was trying to pull the country out of the economic wreckage with a variety of programs he called the New Deal. He put people to work building roads and public buildings, he passed laws that gave people too sick or too old to work enough money to survive.

As a Democrat and a man who had known hard times, Harry Truman vigorously supported these programs. He also showed the same independent streak he had displayed in Missouri. When voters tried to pressure him on various issues, he told them he voted for what he thought was the welfare of the country and he was not governed by threats, pleas, or political considerations.

When a labor leader threatened to order all the members of his union not to vote for him again, Harry Truman told him off in a scorching letter. "It doesn't make any difference to me whether you like the way I vote or not because I vote for what I think is right."

Unfortunately, few voters saw this side of Harry Truman. Because he was elected with the help of boss Tom Pendergast, newspapers called him "the senator from Pendergast" and assumed he voted according to the boss's orders.

Among his fellow senators, Harry Truman soon got a reputation as a worker. He presided over hours of hearings that investigated why so many railroads had gone bankrupt. Again and again, he uncovered evidence that profitable roads had been mismanaged and looted by Wall Street swindlers. They fired thousands of workers, cut maintenance to zero, and neglected badly needed improvements. In a speech on the Senate floor, Senator Truman bluntly denounced these crooks.

> The first railroad robbery was committed on the Rock Island back in 1873. The man who committed the robbery used a gun and a horse and got up early in the morning. That railroad robber's name was Jesse James. About thirty years [later] the Rock Island went through a looting by some gentlemen known as the tin plate millionaires. They used no guns but they ruined the railroad and got away with some seventy million dollars.

The trouble with America, Harry Truman told the Senate, "is that we worship money instead of honor. A billionaire is much greater in the eyes of the people than the public servant who works for the public interest."

After finding out what was wrong with the railroads, Senator Truman went to work on the airlines. They were a mess. Over $120 million had been invested in them and half the money had been lost because the various lines competed recklessly for passengers. They cut fares and skimped on maintenance, which led to numerous crashes. After more hours of hearings, Senator Truman wrote and sponsored the Civil Aeronautics Act, which regulated— but did not eliminate—competition among the airlines, enabling them to begin earning profits.

Along with this hard work, Harry Truman kept in touch with his military interests. He had remained in the National Guard after World War I and had risen to the rank of colonel. Each summer he spent two weeks training in the field. He made many friends from other parts of Missouri in the Guard. One was a shrewd St. Louis banker, John Snyder. Another was a big easygoing joker named Harry Vaughan.

Meanwhile, the world beyond the borders of the United States was drifting toward war. In Italy, a dictator named Benito Mussolini seized power, calling his movement fascism. In Germany, a far more evil man, Adolf Hitler, became the führer (the leader). He called his movement Nazism, and preached hatred of Jews. Defying England and France, Hitler began to rearm Germany and take over small countries on his borders, such as Czechoslovakia and Austria.

Russia was led by Josef Stalin, the head of the Communist party, which had seized power there in 1917. In Japan, military leaders began assassinating civilian politicians, driving out of the government anyone who opposed their plan to conquer China and other Asian countries.

President Roosevelt denounced these movements and urged Americans to join him in preventing a war. But many Americans refused to worry about what the rest of the world was doing. They said the United States had two big oceans between it and Europe and Asia. The newspapers called these Americans isolationists. They formed a committee called America First and opposed the president's attempts to create a united front with France and England, our World War I allies.

Harry Truman supported the president on this issue. His experience in France had convinced him that isolationism was wrong. He had seen the German war machine up close and knew how dangerous it was.

On September 1, 1939, Germany invaded Poland. England and France had a treaty with Poland, promising to defend her against aggression. They declared war on Germany. But they could not stop Hitler's tanks from overrunning Poland in a few weeks.

Because of the world crisis, President Roosevelt decided to run for a third term in 1940. Harry Truman supported him in this decision, too, although many members of the Democratic party, including Truman's vice president, "Cactus Jack" Garner of Texas, opposed him.

That same year, Harry Truman ran for reelection to the Senate. It was a tough fight. Boss Pendergast had been sent to jail for not paying his income tax, and his political machine was in ruins. Worse, President Roosevelt, in spite of Harry Truman's loyal support of his policies, refused to back him. He, too, still seemed to think Truman was the senator from Pendergast.

On his own, Harry Truman ran for reelection against two opponents. He drove around Missouri in one of the hottest summers on record, making hundreds of speeches. No one thought he had a chance, but he amazed the prophets of doom by winning the election. When he returned to Washington, D.C., senators from both parties gave him a standing ovation. No one would ever call him the senator from Pendergast again.

★ ★ ★ ★ ★ ★ ★ 4 ★ ★ ★ ★ ★ ★ ★

From Investigator to President

While Harry Truman was running for reelection in 1940, he watched the next movements of Hitler's army with amazement and dismay. In April of 1940, the Germans overran Denmark and Norway. In May, they smashed into Holland and Belgium, while other panzer divisions, as Hitler's tanks were called, crashed through French defenses in the Ardennes region.

In six incredible weeks, France collapsed and the British army, abandoning tons of equipment, was evacuated from the French port of Dunkirk. Italy joined the war on Germany's side. Winston Churchill, the prime minister of England, vowed to carry on the war—but he warned his people he could offer them nothing but "blood, sweat, and tears."

President Roosevelt responded to this crisis by declaring the United States would become "the arsenal of democracy." At his request, Congress passed a conscription law, drafting men into the army. The United States began to rearm itself, and to export weapons and ammunition to the embattled British. Hitler responded by unleashing the Luftwaffe, his air force, on England, bombing London,

Coventry, and other cities. The British fought back. Their Spitfire pursuit planes inflicted heavy losses on the Germans.

In June of 1941, Hitler attacked Soviet Russia. His armies rampaged through the Russian defenses at first, capturing millions of prisoners as they drove toward Moscow, the capital, and Leningrad, the most important northern city. President Roosevelt did not like the Communist system, but he decided to support the Russians with guns, food, and ammunition, because Hitler's Nazism was worse than communism.

Billions of dollars were being spent to build army camps, to manufacture planes and tanks—and no one was keeping track of the money. After his reelection, Harry Truman decided that the Senate should have a committee to make sure none of the money was being wasted.

President Roosevelt did his best to kill the proposal. He was afraid Truman was going to seek revenge for his refusal to support him for reelection. He feared the committee would dig up mistakes and corruption in the defense program and blame the White House for it.

But Harry Truman remained a loyal Democrat—even if he no longer especially liked Franklin D. Roosevelt. Later in his life, he told a friend that Roosevelt was "the coldest man I ever met. He didn't care about you or me or anyone else in the world." But Truman still considered him a great president.

The Truman committee went to work, despite Roosevelt's opposition. The senator began conducting hearings into the cost of building army camps. He found out that unions were stealing millions through time-and-a-half and double-overtime wage rates. Architects and contractors were earning profits of a thousand percent. In August of 1941, Truman reported that of a billion dollars spent to build the camps, a hundred million dollars had been wasted.

In the fall of 1941, John L. Lewis, the beetlebrowed head of the United States Mine Workers, threatened to call a strike that would have crippled the defense program. Truman summoned Lewis before his committee, where the labor leader discovered he was facing a politician he could not intimidate. When Southern mine owners held out for lower wages for their workers, Truman threatened to call before the committee their real owners, Wall Street's bankers, and reveal that they were a bunch of frauds. The workers got a reasonable pay raise and the brawl was settled without a strike.

Suddenly, a lot of people beyond the borders of Missouri began paying attention to Harry S Truman. Then came an explosion that made him and his committee even more important. On December 7, 1941, Japanese planes attacked the American fleet at Pearl Harbor in Hawaii. The Japanese had a treaty of alliance with Hitler, who soon joined them in declaring war on the United States. World War II now engulfed the entire globe.

More billions were poured into American factories to build ships, tanks, planes, and guns for the American army and America's allies. The Truman committee was busier than ever. But many of his old army friends, such as Harry Vaughan, had rejoined the service. Truman still had soldiering in his blood. He wondered if he could be more helpful to his country in uniform.

He went to see Gen. George Marshall, the army's chief of staff. "I would like very much to work in this war as a field artillery colonel," he said.

Marshall gave Truman a very skeptical look. "How old are you, Senator?" he asked.

"Fifty-six," Truman said.

"You're too damned old," Marshall said. "You'd better stay home and work in the Senate."

"I'm three years younger than you!" Truman said.

"I know," Marshall said. "But I'm already a general."

A lot of men would have marched out of Marshall's office feeling insulted by his bluntness. But Harry Truman filed him away in his mind as a man who said exactly what he thought. He liked that sort of man.

The Truman committee continued its hearings and investigations. Again and again, it uncovered waste and shocking defects in things such as airplane engines and steel plate for warships that would have cost the lives of thousands of American soldiers and sailors. Truman strongly opposed the army's tendency to put colonels in charge of manufacturing programs. He thought civilians could do a better job—and he disliked the army's tendency to sweep mistakes under the rug.

In 1944, Gen. Brehon Somervell, head of army supply, admitted somewhat reluctantly that Truman and his committee had saved the United States $15 billion. Even President Roosevelt tried to get on the Truman bandwagon. "I put him in charge of that war investigating committee," he said, conveniently forgetting how hard he had tried to scuttle the idea.

By 1944, American armies were making headway against Japan and Germany. Italy had already surrendered, although German soldiers still controlled most of the country. On June 6, a huge American-British army landed in France to slug it out with Hitler's panzers. In Russia, the Germans were retreating. Back home in the United States, it was time for another presidential election.

For the Democrats, Franklin D. Roosevelt was the inevitable presidential candidate. But the contest for the vice presidency split the party. Henry Wallace, a former secretary of agriculture, had become vice president when "Cactus Jack" Garner had declined to run with Roosevelt for a third term. Many Democratic leaders did not like Wallace. He was an "issues" man—he liked to spout ideas, but had little ability or interest in dealing with people. His chief support came from labor unions, which made him suspect among Southern Democrats. He was also much too warm an admirer of Soviet Russia.

Insiders also knew that President Roosevelt's health was failing. As one man put it, "We're not nominating a vice president—we're choosing the next president." That made Harry Truman an appealing candidate. Missouri was a border state, so he could attract votes in both the North and South. He was a seasoned politician with many friends in the Democratic party. His work on the Truman committee had given him a national reputation.

The one man who did not share this enthusiasm for making him vice president was Harry Truman. In a letter to his daughter, Margaret, he wrote: "It's funny, how some people would give a fortune to be as close as I am to it and I don't want it. . . . Hope I can dodge it. 1600 Pennsylvania Avenue is a nice address but I'd rather not move in through the back door—or any other door—at sixty."

The reference to the "back door" makes it clear that Harry Truman knew President Roosevelt was a sick man. His knowledge of history made him aware that vice presidents usually have a very difficult time in office. Voters tended to feel that they did not measure up to the president, the man they had really elected to run the country.

The Democratic party convention was in Chicago in 1944. After Roosevelt was nominated, an ugly fight for the vice presidency began. Henry Wallace packed the galleries with his supporters and staged a huge uproar in his favor. But the party's leaders remained committed to Truman. He kept saying he did not want the job. Finally, the Democratic party chairman, Steve Hannegan, a close Truman friend from St. Louis, summoned him to a hotel room to talk on the telephone with Roosevelt, who was in San Diego about to depart on an inspection trip to the Pacific.

"Bob," Roosevelt said, as Truman listened on the line. "Have you got that fellow lined up yet?"

"No," Hannegan said. "He is the contrariest Missouri mule I've ever dealt with."

"Well, you tell him if he wants to break up the Democratic party in the middle of war, that's his responsibility."

Harry Truman was stunned. He realized he had to accept the nomination. "If that is the situation I'll have to say yes," he said. "But why the hell didn't he tell me in the first place?"

As a man from Missouri, the "show-me" state, where people are inclined to speak their minds, Harry Truman found it hard to understand Franklin Roosevelt's fondness for tricky, devious politics.

Back at the convention, the word was passed to the delegates. Truman was running. But on the first ballot, Wallace was ahead by almost a hundred votes. Then several big states, such as New York, switched to Truman. He won in a landslide on the second ballot, 1,031 to 105. Henry Wallace was a very unhappy man.

A month later, Truman met Roosevelt at the White House after he returned from his Pacific trip. The senator was appalled by the president's condition. Roosevelt's hand shook so badly he could not get the cream into his coffee. He talked slowly, sounding like a phonograph running at the wrong speed. He asked Truman how he planned to travel during the campaign.

"I was thinking of using an airplane," Truman said.

Nominated for vice president in 1944, Harry S Truman lunches with President Franklin D. Roosevelt at the White House. Truman left the luncheon aware that the president was a very sick man. He later called him the "coldest man I ever met." But he considered him a "great president." (GEORGE TAMES)

Roosevelt shook his head. "Too dangerous. One of us has to stay alive."

The president knew he was a very sick man. But the election went smoothly. He and his vice president won an easy victory. Immediately after the inauguration, Roosevelt asked Truman to do him a very large favor. He wanted to make Henry Wallace his secretary of commerce. The Senate Democrats, who thought they had gotten rid of Wallace, resisted violently. But Truman used all his political skills to push the appointment through. Little did he realize that he was creating one of his biggest future headaches.

With that political debt paid, Roosevelt sailed off to a final conference with the British and Russians in Yalta. He and Winston Churchill and Josef Stalin discussed the po-

Truman and his family listen to election returns on November 8, 1944, when he won the vice presidency. Left to right are: nephew, Private Fred Truman; sister, Mary Jane Truman; brother, Vivian Truman; wife, Bess Truman; daughter, Margaret; and niece, Martha Ann Truman. (WIDE WORLD PHOTOS)

litical future of Europe. When Roosevelt returned, he was extremely exhausted. He gave a rambling, almost incoherent speech about the Yalta conference to Congress—and never said one word about it to his vice president. In fact, he never discussed any aspect of the war or his relationship with Stalin and Churchill with his vice president.

That was the real reason why the news of President Roosevelt's death came as such a terrible shock to Harry Truman. He realized he was going to have to do one of the fastest catch-up jobs in history.

5

Decisions, Decisions

After he took the oath of office, President Truman asked all the members of President Roosevelt's cabinet to stay in their jobs for the time being. He was interrupted by Steve Early, who said he was being bombarded by reporters who wanted to know if a conference in San Francisco to create the United Nations would meet as planned on April 25.

"Yes!" Truman said in his crispest tone.

The new president told the cabinet members he planned to continue the foreign and domestic policies of the Roosevelt administration. But he also made it clear that he intended to be "president in my own right." He would welcome their opinions—but he was going to make the final decisions.

After the meeting, seventy-eight-year-old secretary of war Henry L. Stimson lingered in the cabinet room. He told the new president that there was one secret he should know immediately. The United States was working on a weapon of enormous explosive power. In the next few days others would tell him more about it.

Most people would have stayed awake for the rest of the night, worrying about this revelation and a thousand and one other details of the ongoing war. But Harry Truman had a unique ability to put worries out of his mind. He also had an inner confidence that he could handle this awesome job he had just inherited. He went back to his two-bedroom apartment on Connecticut Avenue, ate a sandwich and drank a glass of milk, and slept soundly until 6:30 A.M., the time he usually got up.

In the next few days, President Truman learned that the weapon of enormous explosive power mentioned by Secretary of War Stimson was called an atomic bomb. It was being built at a cost of a billion dollars in a secret factory in Tennessee. No one was sure it would work. Admiral William D. Leahy, who was President Roosevelt's chief of staff, called it a "damn-fool thing" and predicted it would never go off.

A report from Maj. Gen. Leslie Groves, the man in direct charge of making the bomb, was more optimistic. He said a test of the bomb was scheduled for the middle of July. A second bomb, which could be used as a weapon against Japan or Germany, would be ready around August 1. General Groves predicted that it would have the power of 1,000 tons of TNT.

Secretary of War Stimson suggested that President Truman should create a committee of experts to consider using the bomb against the enemy. Mr. Truman immediately agreed. At the same time, the president urgently requested from his top diplomats and soldiers an estimate of how much longer they thought the war would last. They told him it would take another six months to conquer Germany, and two more years to defeat Japan.

Newspapers and magazines around the nation were

trying to figure out the new president. A reporter from Kansas City, next door to Mr. Truman's hometown of Independence, Missouri, wrote: "The new president is an average man." *Time* magazine called him "a man of distinct limitations." By some incredible act of hocus-pocus, the press managed to forget all the things Truman had done as head of his investigating committee. They were determined to portray him as a mediocrity.

The story about him that Truman liked best came from a reporter who went out to the family farm and interviewed his mother. He asked Martha Ellen Truman if she was proud of him. "Of course I'm proud of him," she replied. "But I'm just as proud of my son down the road." She was referring to Vivian Truman, who had taken over the farm and was running it with great success.

Meanwhile, Harry Truman went to work as president. On his first day in the White House, he asked Secretary of State Edward Stettinius to give him a report on the country's foreign policy problems. At noon Truman went to the Capitol to dine with seventeen senators and congressmen. Some reporters thought he was just schmoozing with friends. But Truman was already showing his own down-to-earth brand of political leadership. He knew these men. He had worked with them as a legislator. Now he was building a bridge to them from the White House so they would be on his side in the tough times he knew were coming.

Back in the White House that afternoon, the report on foreign policy was on the president's desk. It made grim reading. Relations with Russia had deteriorated badly since the Yalta Conference in February 1945. Already Josef Stalin was breaking promises he had made to permit free elections in the countries of Eastern Europe that the Red

Army had occupied when the Germans retreated. Everywhere Stalin was installing Communist dictatorships, backed by Russian guns.

Truman spent several hours discussing these problems with James Byrnes, the short, balding ex-senator from South Carolina, who had gone to Yalta and earlier summit conferences with President Roosevelt. Deciding he needed someone who knew the history of America's negotiations with the Russians, Truman offered to make Byrnes secretary of state. He accepted instantly—and went off to tell friends that Truman was an ignoramus who would never survive as president without him.

In the next few days, Truman reached out to bring close friends into his administration. Matt Connelly, a shrewd former Truman Committee investigator, became his appointments secretary, a key job. John Snyder, his banker and army friend from St. Louis, became his secretary of the treasury. Charlie Ross, his old high school classmate from Independence, went to work as his press secretary, another key job.

Charlie had become an important Washington reporter for the St. Louis *Post-Dispatch*. They were paying him $35,000 a year—a lot of money in 1945. Harry Truman could only offer him $10,000, but Charlie took the job out of loyalty to his friend. When he came to the White House to tell Truman he accepted the offer, Charlie said: "Won't this be news for Miss Tillie?"

"Let's call her right now," Truman said. "I think it's about time I got that kiss she wouldn't give me on graduation night."

By this time, Miss Tillie Brown was over eighty years old. But she was still living in Independence, and the White House telephone operator found her with no difficulty. "How about that kiss?" Truman asked. "Have I done something worthwhile enough to rate it now?"

"You certainly have," Miss Tillie said.

Miss Tillie was so excited, she called the local paper, the *Independence Examiner*. They called the Associated Press. The next day, the story of the phone call was in every newspaper in the country. Harry Truman began to realize that everything the president does and says is news.

One day he decided to cash a check at his bank. His Secret Service guards looked worried, but they did not try to stop him. Before he had gone a block, Truman realized that a huge crowd was gathering around him. An enormous traffic jam developed as people leapt out of their cars to get a look at the new president. The frantic Secret Service men had to call in the Washington, D.C., police to extricate them and the president from the mob scene. That was President Truman's last stroll to his bank.

But Truman refused to give up his favorite form of exercise—an early-morning walk. Washington reporters, used to covering President Roosevelt, who liked to start the day late, found it hard to get used to the new president's hours.

"At first I thought there might be something of a farm-boy pose in Mr. Truman's early rising," one of them wrote. "That was before I got up at six o'clock for the next three weeks. I began to realize this man *liked* to get up early." The same reporter described Truman's walking speed as "a pace normally reserved for track stars."

On the job, Truman continued to worry about the Russians. They still refused to keep their promises. On April 24, 1945, their foreign minister, V. M. Molotov, came to the White House on his way to the United Nations conference in San Francisco. President Truman began discussing Russian conduct in Poland and Yugoslavia. Molotov answered him with double-talk.

Truman told him that from now on, Russia had to start keeping its promises. He wanted an abrupt stop to treating agreements as a "one-way street."

"I have never been talked to like that in my life!" Molotov said.

"Keep your agreements and you won't get talked to like that," Truman said.

The Russians were among the first to find out that no one pushed President Harry S Truman around.

★ ★ ★ ★ ★ ★ ★ 6 ★ ★ ★ ★ ★ ★ ★

History on the Double

Suddenly things started happening in Europe much faster than any of Truman's military experts had predicted. Instead of lasting six months, Adolf Hitler's evil Nazi regime collapsed in three weeks. German generals surrendered unconditionally to the European commander, Gen. Dwight D. Eisenhower, on May 7. The next day, May 8, was Truman's sixty-first birthday. He broadcast the good news to the nation and wrote a letter to his mother in Missouri asking her: "Isn't that some birthday present?"

While Americans celebrated, President Truman reminded them, "Our victory is only half over." He called on Japan to surrender unconditionally, like Germany. But he tried to reassure the Japanese that the term did not mean extermination of their nation. He told them it would simply mean the end of the influence of military leaders who had brought Japan to the brink of defeat. "It means provision for the return of soldiers and sailors to their families, their farms, their jobs," he said.

Unconditional surrender was an idea that President Roosevelt had announced in 1943. Many people thought it was a mistake. It prolonged the war by making the Germans and Japanese fight more desperately, because they thought the term meant a future of slavery and humiliation.

But the Japanese refused to listen to Truman's plea. They continued to fight Americans on Okinawa. When they could no longer retreat, many of them committed suicide. Hundreds of pilots, called kamikazes, killed themselves by flying planes loaded with bombs into American warships. Thousands of sailors lost their lives. America's military leaders began to think the Japanese could only be defeated by invading their home islands. That would be a bloody, bitter fight.

Meanwhile, Truman flew to San Francisco to launch the United Nations. American and Russian negotiators had wrangled over all sorts of details in putting this organization together. It was supposed to prevent future wars, but the Russians seemed ready to fight a war over everything. They screamed and yelled and pounded on desks, determined to win every argument.

On the way back from San Francisco, Truman ordered the presidential plane, the *Sacred Cow*, to land in Kansas City. He visited his mother in Grandview and then stopped at Eddie Jacobson's haberdashery in Kansas City. Eddie had gone back into business on his own and was very successful.

The president tried to buy some white shirts, but Eddie was embarrassed to reveal that he did not have Truman's size in stock. The story got into the newspapers and thousands of people sent white shirts to the president. He could have started a haberdashery in the White House basement.

In Washington, he submitted the United Nations charter to the Senate for ratification. Everyone wondered if there would be a big blowup. In 1919, Woodrow Wilson had tried to persuade the Senate to ratify the treaty that put the United States in the League of Nations, the organization Wilson had created to prevent wars. But the Republicans—and a few Democrats—had voted against the idea of surrendering America's sovereignty. To everyone's relief, there was practically no opposition to the United Nations.

President Truman was getting some dividends on that lunch he had with his friends in the Senate on his first day in office. In fact, he was able to predict the exact vote—eighty-nine senators for approval, only two against joining the United Nations.

The war in the Pacific continued to rage. On June 17, Truman wrote a memorandum. "I have to decide Japanese strategy. Shall we invade Japan proper or shall we bomb and blockade? That is my hardest decision to date. But I'll make it when I have all the facts."

A few days later, the generals and admirals on the Joint Chiefs of Staff handed him their recommendation for ending the war with Japan. They wanted to begin with an assault on the Japanese home island of Kyushu with 766,700 men. They expected casualties at least as heavy as Okinawa, where 35 percent of the American forces had been killed or wounded. That meant a loss of at least 270,000 men.

After capturing Kyushu, in the spring of 1946, if the Japanese still resisted, the Americans planned to invade the main island, Honshu, and fight a final battle on the plain around Tokyo. Gen. George Marshall predicted at least 500,000 Americans would be killed or wounded in this assault. The Japanese still had an estimated 5,000 planes for their suicide pilots. That meant dozens more smashed and burning American warships.

One of the major reasons

Marshall warned that the number of American casualties would be much higher if the Russians refused to enter the war and pin down the million Japanese soldiers fighting in China. Stalin had promised President Roosevelt he would do so, but so far he seemed more interested in grabbing power in Eastern Europe. That problem made Truman decide he wanted to have a face-to-face talk with the Communist dictator as soon as possible.

Diplomats quickly worked out a meeting with the Russian leader and Winston Churchill at Potsdam, just outside the German capital of Berlin. Truman sailed to Europe on the cruiser USS *Augusta*. He went by train from Antwerp to Potsdam, where Churchill was waiting for him. Stalin was ill and announced he would be a day late.

President Truman and the British prime minister became instant friends. They agreed on all the major issues of the war, particularly the question of getting the Russians to keep their promises. One of Churchill's aides wrote in his diary: "Winston has fallen for the president."

After touring bomb-blasted Berlin, Truman returned to find Secretary of War Stimson very excited. The atomic bomb had been tested in New Mexico and General Groves had said it was a success. The next morning Josef Stalin arrived and the Potsdam Conference began in a beautiful 300-year-old German palace. Stalin suggested that President Truman act as the chairman.

In a letter to his mother, he said the job was as hard as presiding over the Senate, in his brief vice presidency days. "Churchill talks all the time and Stalin just grunts, but you know what he means."

The president had brought along the Joint Chiefs of Staff and he ordered them to confer with Russian generals on a plan to end the war with Japan. Meanwhile, he and Churchill discussed the future of Germany with Stalin. The

President Truman creates a show of unity with Winston Churchill, prime minister of Great Britain, and Josef Stalin, premier of the Soviet Union, at Potsdam in 1945. Truman resisted Stalin's attempt to seize complete control of Germany. In a letter to his mother, the president called it a "nerve-wracking experience." (U.S. ARMY, COURTESY HARRY S TRUMAN LIBRARY)

Russian leader's demands were troublesome. He wanted control of Germany's industrial heartland, the Ruhr. He also wanted some of Italy's former colonies in Africa and "influence" in Syria and Lebanon.

Truman decided these demands were bluffs to conceal Stalin's determination to retain control of Eastern Europe. He concentrated on getting the Russian leader to agree to free elections in Poland. After wrangling all day, Truman returned to his quarters to get the latest report on the atomic bomb. General Groves confirmed that it was the most powerful weapon in history. He estimated it would equal 20,000 tons of TNT. The New Mexico test explosion had been heard 100 miles away.

Here, beyond all doubt, was a weapon that could end the war overnight. At his Potsdam residence, Truman convened a top-level conference to decide whether to use it. He studied the report of the committee of experts Secretary of War Stimson had put together and conferred for hours with his top military advisers. They all recommended the bomb's use, as soon as possible. Truman agreed. It would save millions of lives in the long run.

Truman was thinking of Japanese as well as American lives. Heavy as the American casualties would be in an invasion of Japan, the Japanese, shuddering under a veritable rain of American bombs from planes and shells from warships, would suffer far more. It could easily become a war of extermination.

Churchill agreed with Truman's military and civilian advisers. The bomb should be used quickly "to avoid a vast indefinite butchery." He called it nothing less than "a miracle of deliverance."

That night, Truman went to the map room in his residence, where a young naval officer, George Elsey, was on duty. Solemnly, he wrote out in longhand the order for the first atomic bomb to be dropped as soon as the weather and the readiness of the air crews permitted. But he did not want it dropped until after he left Potsdam. The bomb was still a secret and he did not want to have to answer too many questions about it from the Russians.

The next day, Truman issued a final call for Japan to surrender. Later that day, he told Stalin about the atomic bomb in general terms. He said the United States had developed "a weapon of unusual destructive force." Stalin said he hoped they would use it on the Japanese soon.

The decision made, Truman returned to bargaining with Stalin in a much tougher frame of mind. He no longer thought he needed Russia to win the war. His forceful arguments persuaded the Russian leader to back down on some of his extreme demands for reparations from defeated Germany. The conference ended with a statement that seemed to reflect agreement. But Stalin left in a surly mood, feeling he had been outmaneuvered by the American president.

President Truman returned to America aboard the *Augusta*. On August 6, the fourth day at sea, he decided to have lunch with the crew. He brought his new secretary of state, Jimmy Byrnes, with him. As they sat talking with the sailors, an officer handed Truman a message, reporting the atomic bomb had been dropped on the Japanese city of Hiroshima.

"This is the greatest thing in history," Truman said. He jumped up and told the astonished sailors the news. The men cheered and pounded the tables. He and Byrnes went to the officer's wardroom, where they were eating lunch, and made a similar announcement. The officers cheered as loudly as the enlisted men.

At first, to everyone's amazement, the Japanese did not surrender. They did not believe President Truman's announcement that Hiroshima had been leveled by an atomic bomb. Gen. Leslie Groves, the head of the Manhattan Project, had foreseen this. He had told Truman they would need two bombs to convince the Japanese the war was over.

After three days of stubborn silence from Tokyo, an American B-29 Superfortress dropped a second bomb on the city of Nagasaki. That convinced the Japanese that the atomic bomb was real and the Hiroshima blast was not some sort of accident. The emperor of Japan, Hirohito, offered to make peace—if he could remain on the throne. President Truman agreed to this condition.

The atomic bomb explodes over Hiroshima, Japan, on August 6, 1945. Truman later said he used the bomb to save the lives of millions of Japanese and Americans who would have died in an invasion of Japan. (HARRY S TRUMAN LIBRARY)

By this time, the Russians had joined the war, attacking Japanese armies in Manchuria, China's northern province. Even though Japan's total defeat was obvious, some fanatic military men tried to stage a coup in Toyko, kill the emperor and anyone else who wanted to make peace, and keep fighting. But most of the Japanese accepted the emperor's decision to surrender.

Later, Japanese civilian politicians said that if President Truman had not dropped the two atomic bombs, they could never have negotiated peace. The military fanatics would have killed them. On August 14, President Truman announced that Japan had surrendered unconditionally.

With Mrs. Truman and their daughter, Margaret, the president went out on the north lawn of the White House to greet a huge cheering crowd. Truman flashed the V-for-victory sign with his upraised fingers and went back to the Oval Office to begin a whole new job—leading a nation at peace.

7

★ ★ ★ ★ ★ ★ ★   ★ ★ ★ ★ ★ ★ ★

Politics, Politics, Politics

When the *Augusta* arrived at Norfolk from the Potsdam conference, Truman's old friend John Snyder, his secretary of the treasury, was at the dock, by order of the president. Even then, Truman knew there was no time to waste. The nation urgently needed a plan to convert the American economy from churning out weapons and explosives to making products of peace.

In Potsdam, President Truman had realized that the Russians expected the United States to collapse into another depression as soon as the war ended. They were sure their Communist system was superior—and were calmly preparing to take over Europe and the rest of the world. Truman was determined not to let this happen.

On September 6, the President submitted to Congress a 16,000-word plan to keep America prosperous and strong. It was the longest message any president had sent to Congress since Theodore Roosevelt's day. He proposed government help to build 1.5 million houses, more regional electrical power developments like the Tennessee Valley Authority, a liberal aid program for veterans until they found jobs, and generous loans to small businessmen.

If anyone had any doubts about it, Truman was telling the world that he was president in his own right. The Republicans and conservative Democrats in Congress emitted squawks of rage. They had looked forward to telling Truman how to run the government. Here he was, handing them a twenty-one-point program and telling them to approve it.

Conservative Democrats, mostly from the South, rushed to the White House to protest. Truman told them: "I am the leader of the Democratic party." Toward the end of September, he wrote to his mother: "I've been raising hell. I hate it but it's part of my job."

Beyond Washington, the country was not making a very smooth adjustment to peace. Labor unions were striking for higher wages. Businesspeople wanted an immediate end to wartime price controls, which might stir a roaring inflation. In Washington, Congress balked at Truman's program. Some members of his cabinet, Roosevelt holdovers such as Interior Secretary Harold Ickes, were criticizing the president behind his back.

In war-torn Europe, the specter of starvation stalked the continent. Truman ordered reserves of wheat and corn rushed to France, Germany, England, and Italy. The Russians, at a meeting of foreign ministers in London, were uncooperative about everything. They refused to leave Austria, Iran, and other countries their armies had penetrated.

Worse, Secretary of State James M. Byrnes was acting more and more as if he were the president in everything but name. He declined to send Truman full reports of his meetings with the Russians. The climax to this problem came at the end of 1945, while Truman was spending Christmas in Independence with his family. Byrnes had just returned from a Moscow meeting with the Russians. The president was astonished to learn that the secretary of state was planning to address the American people on the meeting—before reporting to him.

Truman flew to Washington and gave Byrnes a lecture on who was president that made the secretary of state a very apologetic man. Truman also criticized the agreements he had made with the Russians, which permitted them to install puppet governments in Bulgaria, Rumania, and Poland. "I'm tired of babying the Soviets," Truman said.

At the same time another very large international headache—Palestine—began troubling the president. For decades, Jews had been settling there. They were known as Zionists. They believed it was time to regain their ancient biblical homeland. Many more Jews had fled there to escape Nazi persecution. The alarmed Arabs, who had been the majority in the country for over a thousand years, did not like this trend.

Some American Jews urged President Truman to recognize a Jewish state in Palestine immediately. Although he sympathized with their desire to provide a home for the thousands of European Jews in refugee camps, he refused. He had to balance their desires against Arab resentment.

Another problem was China. Russia was keeping a large army in Manchuria. They were also supplying weapons and ammunition to the Chinese Communists, led by Mao Tse-tung. The Americans backed the Nationalist Chinese leader, Chiang Kai-shek, who had been ruling the country when the Japanese invaded it. Truman decided he needed some on-the-spot information. He asked Gen. George Marshall, who had just retired from the army, to go there and give him a thorough report.

With these international problems weighing on his mind, the president struggled to cope with a stew of domestic crises. First the steelworkers, then the autoworkers, then the coal miners, and finally the railroad workers went on strike, threatening to paralyze the country. Truman decided that the nation's welfare was at stake. He respected labor's right to strike—but not in an industry as basic as the railroads.

Truman summoned the head of the railroad union and the chief negotiator for management to the White House. At the same time he sent a bill to Congress, asking for the power to draft workers to keep the railroads running. The two sides settled, but the head of the union left the White House vowing that he would spend the union's entire $47-million treasury to defeat Truman for reelection.

Truman knew he was in trouble. He wrote to his sister: "The Republicans and the crackpot Democrats have started out on an organized campaign to discredit me for their own selfish ends."

Meanwhile, more troubling news flowed into the White House from abroad. The American general in command of U.S. forces in Korea warned that the Russians were trying to install a Communist government. In France, another general asked for instructions if the Communists attempted an armed takeover of the government. In Eastern Europe, the Russians were executing and jailing anyone who resisted their puppet regimes.

While world tension mounted, Truman took a trip to Missouri with his friend Winston Churchill. The ex–prime minister—he had been voted out of power—had been invited to speak at Westminster College in the "show-me" state. En route, Churchill announced he would like to play a few hands of American poker. Truman was very good at this game—and several people in his entourage, such as his military aide, his old friend Gen. Harry Vaughan, were even better.

As the train rumbled west, they started to play. They soon realized that Churchill simply did not understand the game. They could have taken him for every cent in his pockets. But on orders from the president, they allowed Winston to win enough money to make him feel he was one of the boys.

In Missouri Churchill made a historic speech. With Truman in the audience, he declared that an "iron curtain" had fallen across Europe, dividing free men from those enslaved by Communist tyranny. He called on England and America to remain strong to resist Russian aggression. "There is nothing for which they have less respect than military weakness," he said.

Because Truman was present, many people thought he agreed with Churchill. But a few days later, he wrote to his mother: "I am not yet ready to endorse Mr. Churchill's speech." In spite of disappointments, he still hoped to reach an agreement with Moscow that would establish a secure and peaceful world. To prove it, he invited Stalin to visit the United States for a face-to-face negotiation. The Soviet dictator curtly refused, claiming that his doctor forbade it.

This gesture did not satisfy some of Truman's critics in the Democratic party. Their leader was the man he had defeated for the vice presidency in Chicago, Henry Wallace. He was still a member of the cabinet, Truman's secretary of commerce. But that did not stop him from accusing Truman of being responsible for the growing hostility between the United States and Russia.

Truman called Wallace to the White House for a talk. He warned him that he could not stay in his administration if he made such accusations. Wallace pretended to be apologetic. He took out a speech he was planning to make in New York and asked if Truman approved it. The president glanced through it. The key phrase was, "I am neither anti-British nor pro-British, neither anti-Russian nor pro-Russian." Truman agreed with that idea and said he was pleased to see Wallace was getting closer to his point of view.

Wallace went to New York and made a completely different speech—violently attacking those who criticized Russia—and announced it had Truman's approval. It was a classic double cross, making Truman look foolish. At that very moment, Secretary of State Byrnes was in Moscow taking a tough line toward the Russians. The gleeful Republicans wanted to know who was in charge of America's foreign policy.

Once more, Truman called Wallace to the White House—and he promised to make no more speeches on foreign policy. On his way out he met some reporters and started making a speech on the White House steps. Truman decided he was hopeless and asked for his resignation. But he knew that he had not heard the last of Wallace. There were quite a few Democrats who agreed with him.

All this turmoil in the Democratic party, plus rising prices in the grocery stores and clothing stores, and a lot of veterans still unemployed meant trouble in the 1946 congressional elections. Democrats were swept out of office by the dozens. For the first time in sixteen years, Republicans gained control of both houses of Congress.

The Democratic Congress had refused to support Truman's twenty-one-point program. Many of their members, such as Senator Claude Pepper of Florida, had frequently backed Henry Wallace's pro-Russian foreign policy. But they promptly blamed the debacle on President Truman. Senator William J. Fulbright of Arkansas, a Democrat, suggested that Truman appoint a Republican secretary of state, then resign, so the Republican could become president.

It was a good thing Harry Truman was used to Washington politics. He called this kind of idiocy "Potomac fever." When one of his cabinet members, Secretary of the Navy James Forrestal, suggested he try to create a nonpartisan committee that would help him work with Congress, Truman gently rejected the idea. He told Forrestal that the name of the game in Washington always was and always would be politics. Now was the time to start playing it for keeps.

President Truman welcomes his mother, Martha Ellen Truman, to Washington for a White House visit. An unreconstructed Confederate sympathizer, she refused to sleep in Lincoln's bed. (J. SHERREL LAKEY, COURTESY HARRY S TRUMAN LIBRARY)

8

At Home in the White House

While President Truman dealt with the immense problems of the war-wracked world and the infuriating headaches of domestic politics, he struggled to remain plain Harry Truman, a devoted husband, father, son, and brother. Early in May 1945, he invited his mother, sister, Mary, and brother, Vivian, to visit him in the White House.

Martha Ellen Truman was her usual outspoken self. When she saw all the reporters waiting for her to get off the plane, she said: "Why didn't you tell me there was going to be all this fuss? If I'd known, I wouldn't have come."

Margaret, who loved to tease everyone in the family, told Mamma Truman she was going to sleep in Abraham Lincoln's bed. Mrs. Truman's family had been strong supporters of the Confederacy in the Civil War and she remained "unreconstructed," as the president liked to say. She announced that she would sleep on the floor before she slept in Lincoln's bed.

The president shushed his daughter and told his mother she was going to sleep in the Rose Room, where

President Truman arrives at Kansas City Municipal Airport to be greeted by his sister, Mary Jane Truman, and his brother, Vivian Truman. He wrote regularly to them while he was in the White House. (KANSAS CITY STAR)

visiting queens stayed. But Mamma Truman decided the bed was too "grand" for her. She slept next door in a smaller room, and left the Rose Room to her daughter, Mary.

Harry Truman's ingrained sense of equality made him uneasy about being waited on by the dozens of White House servants. He and Bess Truman made a point of knowing each one by name. When the family sat down to dinner during Mamma Truman's visit, Truman introduced his brother, Vivian, to Alonzo Fields, the head butler. Vivian shook hands with him, astonishing the rest of the staff. They were used to waiting on VIPs who barely recognized that they existed.

Whenever a new man was added to the dining room staff, Fields introduced him to the president. Truman would shake hands with him and say: "Now, don't be disturbed by me. We're glad to have you aboard."

Teasing each other was a basic part of the Truman tradition, and they did not let the White House atmosphere slow them down. The president loved to pick out the loudest tie he could find and wear it to breakfast, evoking cries of horror and outrage from Margaret and Bess.

One night Margaret invited two friends to spend the night with her in Lincoln's bedroom. Truman cooked up a plan with Mayes, one of the butlers, to scare them silly. Mayes was tall and thin; in poor light he resembled Lincoln. Truman wanted to put a high hat on Mayes's head and send him into the bedroom as Lincoln's ghost. Unfortunately, Mayes had no enthusiasm for the job and arranged not to be on duty that night.

Bess Truman was a reluctant first lady. An extremely private person, she disliked the constant publicity, the perpetual presence of the Secret Service, and the lack of privacy. But she tackled the job with determination and soon won the respect of the Washington diplomatic corps and the press. "First ladying," as Margaret called it, was hard work. The regular White House social program involved formal dinners, teas, and receptions. Toward the close of the 1946 social season, Bess wrote to Margaret: "These [next] two weeks are going to be a handshaking two weeks—conservative estimate forty-one hundred."

Both the president and his wife were determined to make sure twenty-one-year-old Margaret lived a reasonably normal life. Each summer, Bess took her back to Independence for several months, where she was out of the glare of White House publicity. Truman missed her intensely and when she failed to answer his numerous letters, she would get sarcastic inquiries: "Is your arm paralyzed?"

Early in 1946, Margaret informed her parents that she wanted to be a professional singer. It was something she had dreamed about since girlhood and she did not see why she should give it up because her father had become president. Truman pointed out to her the possibility that she would become the target of malicious critics, who were really attacking him as president. That only aroused what Margaret called her "Truman determination."

Once she decided to go ahead with her ambition, the president gave her his wholehearted support. He offered her only one piece of advice: "Don't become a temperamental case. . . . It makes no friends, and to succeed at anything you must have friends on whom you can rely.

Margaret Truman launched a successful singing career in 1947. Here she performs in Denver with flutist Lib Knowland. She has since become a writer. (ASSOCIATED PRESS/WIDE WORLD PHOTO)

This is just as true of a musical career as it is of a political one."

Truman arranged an interview with one of the stars of the Metropolitan Opera, who was very encouraging. He said Margaret would have to work hard and train under professional direction, but he was convinced she had the basic vocal equipment to succeed. The president was delighted by the news. At the end of a warm letter, he added a typically Trumanesque touch: "You'd better tell me what your expenses are to date. We don't want to be charity patients of anybody."

On March 16, 1947, Margaret made her professional debut with the Detroit Symphony Orchestra. As she put it in her lively way, the entire Truman administration was glued to the radio at 8:28 Eastern Standard Time. She had barely recovered from a bout of bronchial pneumonia, but she summoned her Truman determination and sang beautifully.

She was heartened by a letter from her father: "Nothing can stop you. Not even the handicap of being the daughter of President Truman!"

Thousands of letters poured into the White House from all over the nation, expressing the public's enthusiasm for Margaret's performance. Other singers, such as opera star Robert Merrill, sent praise and encouragement. She also received an offer to star in a film named *Las Vegas*.

Margaret turned that down without even bothering to ask her father. "I knew what he would say," she said.

Soon Margaret was touring the country on the concert circuit. In Washington, D.C., the president complained about how lonely he was in "the Great White Jail."

★ ★ ★ ★ ★ ★ ★ **9** ★ ★ ★ ★ ★ ★ ★

Push Comes to Shove, at Home and Abroad

Before President Truman could start playing hardball politics with the Republican Congress, another international crisis exploded in his face. The British informed him that they were running out of money and could no longer pay for the military aid they were giving Greece to help them fight off a Russian-backed assault by Communist rebels.

A few days later, Turkey reported that she was close to bankruptcy because she had to maintain a 600,000-man army to resist Russian pressure to give them control of the straits of the Bosporus at the entrance to the Black Sea. Truman had to act—and act fast.

He went before Congress and asked for $400 million in aid to Greece and Turkey to help them resist totalitarianism. Nowhere in his speech did he mention Russia by name. But everyone knew what the president was talking about. In fact, by identifying communism with totalitarianism, Truman won an instant propaganda victory. America had just fought a war to free Europe and Asia from German and Japanese totalitarianism. He was telling people that communism was basically the same thing—a system that denied fundamental freedoms to its citizens.

Wallace's followers in Congress tried to torpedo the president's policy. But the Republican party proved remarkably agreeable to Truman's ideas. It was the beginning of a historic shift in which the Republicans abandoned isolationism.

The decision to support allies menaced by Communist aggression became known as the Truman Doctrine. Although the aid package for Greece and Turkey was hammered out in three frantic weeks, Truman was operating with a game plan, thanks to some remarkable foresight by him and others in the administration. In the summer of 1946, he asked the White House counsel, Clark Clifford, and his assistant, George Elsey (the same man who had transmitted Truman's order to drop the atomic bomb), to prepare a position paper to clarify their policy with Russia.

This study concluded that Russia's relationship with the United States would remain hostile for a long time, because the Communists believed there was an inevitable conflict between their system and capitalism. But Clifford and Elsey concluded that the Russians did not want to start a war. There was some hope that eventually they could be persuaded to be reasonable. But only if the United States firmly resisted their attempts to encroach on the free world.

On the domestic front, President Truman found himself in frequent clashes with the Republican Congress. Probably the biggest brawl was over their passage of the Taft-Hartley Act, which tried to limit the power of unions and generally favor the management side in labor relations. President Truman vetoed it, but Congress overrode his veto by two-thirds majorities in both houses, and it became law.

In spite of this domestic conflict, Truman was able to work with the Republican Congress on another foreign policy triumph. At the 1947 Harvard graduation, Gen. George Marshall, who had replaced Jimmy Byrnes as secretary of state, announced the largest aid program in the history of the world.

Truman and his advisers had been working on the proposal for months. Their representatives in Europe had reported that every country on the continent was an economic basket case. Even England, once the world's strongest economy, was sinking into poverty. In this atmosphere of defeat and disarray, communism was sure to flourish.

Clark Clifford suggested the program should be called The Truman Plan.

"Are you crazy?" the president said. "If we sent that up to the Republican Congress with my name on it, they'd tear it apart. We're going to call it the Marshall Plan."

The Marshall Plan was what it became. Sixteen European nations met in Paris and drew up a statement of their needs. On November 17, 1947, Truman told an astonished Congress that he wanted $17 billion to make it work—with $6.8 billion needed by April 1, 1948. The president and his staff worked day and night for weeks to put together arguments to convince the lawmakers that the American economy could raise and loan such a staggering sum.

"I've had the most terrible and terrific ten days since April 12, 1945," Truman told his daughter, Margaret. "I've worked from sunup to sundown and a couple of hours before and five after every day."

To dramatize his request, the president called a special session of Congress and worked closely with old friends such as Arthur Vandenberg, the Republican senator from Michigan. From abroad came a savage Russian reaction. Stalin sent orders to Communist leaders in Italy and France to seize power before the Marshall Plan started. In Greece, the Americans had to commit B-29 bombers to beat back a Communist offensive. From Berlin, Gen. Lucius Clay flashed a warning: "War may come with dramatic suddenness."

At home Henry Wallace and his supporters attacked the Marshall Plan with equal savagery, claiming it was a covert declaration of war on the Russians. It seems incredible today, when we know that this idea rescued Europe from collapse, to realize that these men and women managed to convince themselves that it was a mistake to try to help fellow democracies, simply because it offended one of the great mass murderers of history, Josef Stalin.

In spite of threats from abroad and criticism at home, Harry Truman stayed on his chosen course. In March of 1948, he flew to New York to address the Friendly Sons of St. Patrick. He drew on his knowledge of history to defend his policy, saying, "We must not be confused about the issue which confronts the world today. The issue is as old as recorded history. It is tyranny against freedom. . . ."

Truman knew that pumping money into Europe's economy was not going to stop the Russians. They only understood the language of force. Soon after he launched the Marshall Plan, he asked Republican senator Arthur H. Vandenberg to help him create a military alliance between the United States and the free nations of Europe. Truman called it the North Atlantic Treaty Organization.

This was political dynamite. In his farewell address, President George Washington had warned Americans against making "entangling alliances." He had been worried about the great powers of that time sucking the weak United States into their wars. Now the United States was the most powerful nation on earth, but President Truman saw that we needed allies to help us defeat communism. He persuaded the Senate to go along with him, inch by patient inch, with Vandenberg's support a crucial factor. On June 11, 1948, the Senate voted its approval by an astonishing 64–4. Senator Vandenberg called it "the most important step in American foreign policy since the promulgation of the Monroe Doctrine."

Meanwhile, the Palestinian time bomb began ticking again. The British, who ruled the Holy Land under a United Nations mandate, announced that they could no longer pay the cost of maintaining 90,000 troops to keep peace between the Arabs and the Jews. Jewish guerrillas had begun attacking their troops. They were pulling out. Truman's old friend, Eddie Jacobson, came to the White House to speak on behalf of American Jews, urging Truman to recognize a Jewish state. Truman sternly told him he could not let friendship influence such a major decision.

In June of 1948, Stalin pulled his dirtiest trick yet. He clamped a blockade on all train and truck traffic to Berlin. Germany had been divided into East Germany, where the Russians had installed a Communist government, and West Germany, where democracy was beginning to flourish. Berlin, the old capital of united Germany, was deep inside East German territory. But it was a free city, divided into U.S., British, French, and Russian zones. Stalin hoped he could force the Allies to make a humiliating retreat from this symbol of German identity.

Instead, President Truman started an airlift. Day after

day, hundreds of planes flew supplies to the 2 million citizens of West Berlin. The Russians did not know how to stop them. It took another ten months, but finally the Russians gave up and lifted the land blockade. Once more, Harry Truman had demonstrated that nobody pushed him around. He had also given the world a brilliant example of how to resist Russian aggression without starting a war.

Meanwhile, the turmoil in Palestine mounted. Truman was under terrific pressure from American Jewish voters to back the formation of an independent state. They sent 86,500 letters, 841,003 postcards, and 51,400 telegrams to the White House, stating their position. The U.S. State Department diplomats strongly opposed a Jewish state, and they convinced General Marshall, the secretary of state, to side with them. The Russians, eager as always to embarrass the United States, announced that they favored a Jewish state. This was pure hypocrisy. Josef Stalin was almost as anti-Semitic as Adolf Hitler.

The State Department favored replacing the British mandate with a United Nations trusteeship. President Truman, after long and serious thought, decided to support an independent Jewish state. He agreed that the need for such a refuge had been made clear by Hitler's slaughter of 6 million Jews during World War II. This conclusion brought on a crisis with General Marshall that required all Truman's political skills to resolve. Only the general's deep loyalty to the idea that the president was the leader of the nation kept him in the cabinet.

On May 14, the day before the British pulled out of Palestine, Israel declared itself a state. Eleven minutes later, President Truman issued a statement through his press secretary, Charlie Ross, granting them U.S. recognition. Bitter fighting with Arab armies exploded across

Palestine. It soon became clear that Israel would survive—and Truman's recognition was a decisive factor in that survival.

During these same early months of 1948, Harry Truman stirred up another political storm by sending to Congress the most far-reaching civil rights program in American history. He called on city and state governments and the federal government to join in closing "a serious gap between our ideals and our practices." Black Americans were being treated as second-class citizens, forced to live behind walls of legal segregation which condemned them to inferior education, jobs, and social lives.

The president called for the establishment of a Fair Employment Practices Commission and a civil rights division in the Department of Justice. He wanted better protection for black voters in the South. He backed the desegregation of the armed forces with executive order 9981, which called on the army, navy, and air force to integrate their ranks as soon as possible.

Truman knew that the southern Democrats in Congress would be infuriated by this program, but he went ahead with it. When a reporter asked him where he had gotten his ideas, he replied: "The Constitution, containing the Bill of Rights, was the only document considered in the writing of that message."

The southern Democrats' fury was so intense, many people feared the party was about to collapse into fragments, as it had done in 1860, on the eve of the Civil War. They went to the White House to plead with Truman to soften his views. The president shook his head. He told them that his mother and all his relatives of her generation had sympathized with the South in the Civil War. Jim Crow segregation was as widespread in Missouri as it was in Alabama.

Emotionally, as a single individual named Harry Truman, he might be inclined to soften his program. But he was also president of the United States—and as president, he could not do it. He told his visitors that "my very stomach turned" when he learned that black soldiers, just back from overseas, had been dumped out of trucks in Mississippi and beaten by whites to make sure they did not become "uppity."

"Whatever my inclinations as a native of Missouri might have been, as president I know this is bad. I shall fight to end evils like this," Harry Truman said.

10

The Loneliest Campaign

In spite of his courage and his achievements in foreign policy, a lot of people did not think Harry Truman was doing a good job as president. These included a large number of Democrats. The followers of Henry Wallace were talking about running Wallace for president as the candidate of the Progressive party. The southern Democrats were also threatening to run a separate candidate. The leading political columnist of the *New York Times* declared: "The president's influence is weaker than any president's has been in modern history."

Other Democrats, including several sons of Franklin D. Roosevelt, looked to Gen. Dwight D. Eisenhower as their savior. They approached the former Allied supreme commander, who had retired from the army and was serving as president of Columbia University in New York. They told him the Democratic party's nomination was his for the asking. President Truman watched these maneuvers and was not amused. No one had asked him the crucial question: Was he going to run for another term?

For a while he was undecided. Writing to his sister,

Mary, early in 1948, he made it clear that he was proud of his presidency so far. "Many decisions have had to be made—most of them of worldwide significance. . . . They've almost all been right and when history is written without prejudice it will say just that."

At the same time, he was not exactly dazzled by many aspects of his job. "I'm rather fed up on all the folderol it takes to be president," he told his sister. "If it were not for the world situation and my lack of confidence in the presidential candidates, I'd throw the whole works out the window and go home and stay there."

As Truman saw it, Henry Wallace wanted to hand over the world to Josef Stalin & Company. The southern Democrats, who were calling themselves Dixiecrats, did not care what happened beyond their states' borders. The Republican candidate, Thomas E. Dewey, the governor of New York, was a colorless man with no foreign policy experience.

So Harry Truman made up his mind to seek another four years in the White House. "I can't run from responsibility, as you know," he told his sister. "So I have to face the music. Europe, China, Palestine, terrible Russia, and the special privilege boys here at home."

Truman's first priority was squelching the Eisenhower boom. He told his secretary of defense, James Forrestal, to call Ike and ask him if he was a candidate. Ike said no. Forrestal told him to make a public statement to that effect, and the gas fizzled out of that trial balloon.

Nevertheless, when the Democratic Convention met on July 12, 1948, the atmosphere was gloomy. The Dixiecrats were still threatening to bolt from the party. One of them paid Harry Truman an inadvertent compliment in the middle of his threats. A reporter asked him why he was so excited about Truman's civil rights program. President Roosevelt had included a promise to fight for civil rights in the Democratic party's platform every time he ran. "I know," said the Dixiecrat. "But Truman means it!"

On July 14, the Dixiecrats proved they meant it, too. When the convention voted in favor of the Truman civil rights program, the southerners walked out and nominated Strom Thurmond of South Carolina for president.

That night, Truman arrived in Philadelphia to accept the party's nomination. It was hot, humid weather. The delegates were wilted by the heat and discouraged by the party's internal feuds. They wasted hours wrangling over the vice presidential nomination before finally giving it to Senator Alben Barkley of Kentucky. Not until 1:45 A.M. was Harry Truman escorted to the convention floor to accept the nomination for president.

Trying to create peace with a symbol, someone unleashed a flock of doves from inside a fake Liberty Bell. While the band played "Hail to the Chief," the traditional presidential welcoming song, the birds swirled groggily around the smoke-filled convention hall. One almost landed on Speaker of the House Sam Rayburn's head while he was trying to introduce President Truman.

Another dove crashed into an upper balcony and plummeted to the convention floor. A wise-guy reporter looked at the dead bird and said: "There lies Harry S Truman."

The president ignored this silly sideshow. He strode to the lectern and gazed sternly at the soggy, weary crowd. Wearing a crisply pressed white suit, he looked as fresh and energetic as he did on his morning walks. "Senator Barkley and I are going to win this election and make those Republicans like it—don't you forget that," he said.

The confident words went through the convention hall

like a bolt of electricity. Suddenly Democrats were on their feet, screaming with enthusiasm. For the next twenty minutes, Harry Truman told them why he was so sure of victory. He lambasted the Republican-controlled 80th Congress for its attacks on labor and surrenders to special interests. He cited the gains working men and their families had made in the booming postwar prosperity.

Then came a total surprise. To make sure these gains were not lost, Truman announced that he was going to call a special session of Congress to enact parts of his program the Republicans had ignored. "On the 26th of July, which out in Missouri we call Turnip Day, I am going to call Congress back and ask them to pass laws to halt rising prices, to meet the housing crisis, and act upon other vitally needed measures."

Pandemonium almost lifted the roof off the convention hall as the delegates roared their approval. Harry Truman was showing the Democrats—and the nation—how much he had learned about leadership from his study of America's political history.

Even columnist Max Lerner, who had been deploring the convention as a political vacuum, changed his mind about Harry Truman. "It was a great speech for a great occasion," he wrote. "I found myself applauding."

The president's morale got a boost—if it needed it— from his friend Winston Churchill, who sent him a copy of the first volume of his history of World War II, *The Gathering Storm.* "I greatly admire your conduct of international affairs in Europe during your tenure of the most powerful office in the world," he wrote in an accompanying note.

In spite of these hopeful omens, the polls showed that Truman was still far behind the Republican candidate,

Thomas E. Dewey. Later in July, the president called his aides into the Oval Office to discuss the upcoming campaign. Truman sensed a mood of discouragement. Someone wondered if all they could do was put up a good fight.

The president instantly changed the atmosphere with another injection of confidence. "We are going to win," he said. "I expect to travel all over the country and talk at every whistle-stop. It's going to be tough on everybody, but that's the way it's got to be."

Charlie Ross, Truman's old friend and press secretary, often said in later years that the president won the election that day, though it was not visible at the time. Truman's campaign lacked money for travel expenses and advertising. He was being attacked by Henry Wallace as a warmonger and by the Dixiecrats as an enemy of white supremacy. The Republican candidate, Thomas E. Dewey, dismissed him as an incompetent.

The Republican Congress gathered for their Turnip Day session in an extremely bad mood. They rejected every proposal Truman sent to them as "the last hysterical gasp of an expiring administration." They ignored his call to extend Social Security protection and other measures to help the average man and woman. "They are trying to blame me because they did nothing," Truman told his sister. "I just don't believe the people can be fooled that easily."

True to his word, Harry Truman and his staff took to the rails in a tour that crisscrossed the country twice, stopping at small towns and large cities along the way. At every stop, Truman would come out on the observation platform of the last car on the train, introduce Mrs. Truman and his daughter, Margaret, and attack the 80th Congress. Occasionally he would get off the train and speak on the radio, which was still the best way to reach large numbers of people. Television sets were just beginning to appear in American homes.

The president's campaign was so short of money, several times the networks cut Truman off in midsentence when he reached the end of the air time he had paid for. They did not seem to realize that many people considered this an insult to the office of the presidency as well as to the man.

On October 11, 1948, one of Truman's aides jumped off the train to buy a copy of *Newsweek*. The magazine had polled fifty political experts around the country on who would win the election. Every single one predicted a Dewey victory. Morale on the train plummeted—except for the president's. He tossed the magazine aside and told Clark Clifford, the White House counsel: "I know every one of those fifty fellows and not one of them has enough sense to pound sand down a rathole."

On October 13, two days after *Newsweek*'s experts had prophesied his rout, Truman told George Elsey that he was sure he would win—and predicted how many electoral votes he and his opponents would get. He saw himself winning 340 votes, Dewey 108, Dixiecrat Strom Thurmond 42, and Wallace, zero.

All the polls still showed the president far behind Dewey. No one seemed to notice that at stop after stop, the crowds that came out to see Truman were getting larger. He continued to attack the Republicans from all points of the compass. Instead of "Grand Old Party," the initials G.O.P. really meant "Gluttons Of Privilege," Truman said.

Again and again, President Truman showed how well he could talk to ordinary people. Speaking to farmers in

Dexter, Iowa, he told them, "I can plow a straight furrow. A prejudiced witness said so: my mother." When a woman in California told him he sounded as if he had a cold, he replied: "That's because I ride around in the wind with my mouth open."

Another time he demonstrated his coolness in an emergency. A boy rode a skittish horse to the edge of a crowd in Oklahoma. President Truman climbed down from the observation platform and grabbed the bridle. "That's a fine horse you've got there, son," he said. He led the horse over to his Secret Service men, who made sure it stayed a safe distance from the crowd.

While Truman was getting through to the people, his opponents were self-destructing. Henry Wallace compared Communists to early Christians—which showed how much he know about Josef Stalin, the murderer of an estimated 50 million people. Outside the Deep South, no one was interested in Strom Thurmond. Tom Dewey was so sure he was going to win, he went out of his way to say as little as possible in his speeches—reducing his audiences to terminal boredom.

In his final speech of the campaign, in St. Louis, Truman gave Dewey a farewell blast. "Of all the fake campaigns, this one is tops as far as the Republican candidate for president is concerned," he said.

Back in-Independence on November 2, Truman voted at 10:00 A.M. Reporters asked him if he was going to sit up late to hear the returns from around the country. "No," the president said. "I think I'll go to bed. I don't expect final results until tomorrow."

On that election day, Drew Pearson, one of Washington's best-known columnists, wrote that Dewey had conducted "one of the most skillful campaigns in recent history." He devoted his column to the likely members of

Dewey's cabinet. Another famous columnist, Walter Lipp-mann, predicted a total Democratic disaster from which the party might never recover.

Later in the day, Truman slipped away to a hotel in the small town of Excelsior Springs, about twenty-five miles from Independence. Repeating his performance on the night he became president, he ate a ham sandwich, drank a glass of milk, and went to bed early. While he slept soundly, the votes began coming in. To everyone's amazement, the president was ahead of Dewey. He stayed that way for the rest of the night, while various broadcasters tried to explain it away.

Just as Truman had predicted, the final result was not

In 1948 *The Chicago Tribune* was so confident Truman would lose the presidential election that they printed a first edition with the Republican candidate, Thomas E. Dewey, proclaimed the winner. Here, the day after the election, a grinning Truman displays a copy from his campaign train. (MERCANTILE LIBRARY ASSOCIATION)

clear until the following morning. In 1948, millions of ballots had to be counted by hand. At 11:14 A.M. Dewey conceded defeat, after Truman had carried California, Ohio, and Illinois, giving him 304 electoral votes. This was only 37 votes short of the number he predicted to George Elsey on October 13.

On the way back to Washington, someone came aboard the campaign train with a copy of the November 3 *Chicago Tribune*. The paper had been one of Truman's toughest critics. The editors were so confident that he was going to lose, they had printed their first edition with a huge black headline: "Dewey Defeats Truman." A grinning president held it up when the train stopped along the route.

In Washington, D.C., a gigantic crowd cheered the reelected president. At least a dozen bands played "I'm Just Wild about Harry." On the front of the Washington *Post* building hung a huge sign: "Mr. President, We Are Ready to Eat Crow Whenever You Are Ready to Serve It."

Not only had Harry Truman won reelection—he had carried a Democratic majority into Congress with him. From now on, he was president in his own right. And then some.

Wild Party

A few days after his reelection, Harry Truman headed for his favorite vacation spot, the U.S. Navy submarine base at Key West. Converting the commandant's quarters into a miniature White House, he wandered around in a pith helmet and various tropical shirts, handing out cards that said: "Don't go away mad. Just go away."

He played practical jokes on all comers. Anyone foolish enough to take a nap on the beach would get a pitcher of ice water poured on his stomach, courtesy of the president. One day Truman joined the daily press conference, equipped with pad and pencil, and started asking the reporters pointed questions, such as when they went to bed the previous night. He knew most of them had been partying until dawn.

Occasionally he went fishing with his aides and Mrs. Truman, but he rarely caught anything. Mrs. Truman was an expert fisherman and usually caught more than anyone else on the boat. Truman's favorite sport was talking history. One day he began discussing military history with one of his aides. Using four settings of silverware in place

Truman relaxed with his daughter, Margaret, and his staff after the 1948 campaign at his favorite vacation spot, the navy's submarine base in Key West, Florida. Practical jokes and wildly colored shirts were the order of the day. The president gave out cards saying: "Don't go away mad. Just go away." (U.S. NAVY, COURTESY HARRY S TRUMAN LIBRARY)

of toy soldiers, he proceeded to give the blow-by-blow story of the thirteen major battles in the history of the world. The astonished aide said Truman was so far ahead of the professors he had in college, there was "no comparison."

Truman carefully avoided gloating over his astonishing election victory. "Let's be generous and make 'em like it," he told everyone. But to his sister, Mary, he could not resist expressing a little private delight. All over the country, he told her, newspapers were "banqueting on crow."

From Winston Churchill came a letter telling him

"what a relief it has been to me and most of us here" in England to learn that he had won the election. It seemed to the great Englishman "the best chance of preserving peace."

Back in Washington, Truman found he had to move out of the White House after all. Not because he had lost the election, but because the 150-year-old mansion was about to fall down. No major repairs had been made on it for decades. "The engineer told me the ceiling in the state dining room stayed up only from force of habit!" Truman wrote to his sister. He and his family moved around the corner to a smaller mansion, Blair House.

Meanwhile, everyone was getting ready for the inauguration on January 20. Truman made sure it was quite a party. He started the day by having breakfast with ninety-eight members of his World War I battery and their wives. Then Captain Harry issued marching orders. They were to escort his car in the inaugural parade up Pennsylvania Avenue. He wanted them to maintain their old army pace, 120 thirty-inch steps per minute.

Once more, dozens of bands played "I'm Just Wild about Harry." On this day of days, almost everyone meant it. Only the Dixiecrats frowned and growled when Truman issued an order making this the first inauguration in American history that was completely integrated. Black and white Americans marched together in the parade, danced and ate together at the parties. The head of the National Association for the Advancement of Colored People praised the president for "recognizing the new place of all ordinary Americans."

In his inaugural address to the nation, Truman told his fellow Americans that they were facing an uncertain world, in which democracy was being attacked by a false philosophy, communism. He summed up the differences between the two ideas in a few simple words.

> Communism is based on the belief that man is so weak and inadequate, he is unable to govern himself and therefore requires the rule of strong masters.
>
> Democracy is based on the conviction that man has the moral and intellectual capacity, as well as the inalienable right, to govern himself with reason and justice.

To win the struggle, the United States had to assume the leadership of the free world, Truman said. It had to do four things: 1) continue to support the UN; 2) continue to support the Marshall Plan; 3) give military help to nations resisting Communist aggression; 4) do something about improving the whole world.

More than half the people on Earth were living in poverty. Truman proposed a bold new program to share America's technological and scientific skills to help people change their lives. Reporters called the idea Point Four—and it swept around the world, igniting hope in struggling Egyptian farmers, Greek fishermen, Irish craftspeople. Hundreds of young Americans rushed to volunteer for the program. Soon more than 2,000 of them would travel to Indonesia, Iran, Kenya, to teach people how to raise more food, purify their water, improve their schools.

Harry S Truman was the first political leader to urge the rich nations to aid the world's poor. English historian Arnold Toynbee said it would be remembered as "the signal achievement of the age."

For the moment, Americans remembered Harry Truman's inauguration as the best party they had seen in a long time. The people who had the most fun were the members of Battery D. They obeyed the president's order

Point Four volunteers at work in Peru, demonstrating the latest agricultural methods. President Truman announced this program to share Western science and technology with the poorer nations of the world in his 1948 inaugural address. (COURTESY HARRY S TRUMAN LIBRARY)

and managed to keep going at 120 steps a minute for the mile-and-a-half march. But at the inaugural ball that night, some of them had sore feet. "The Germans never came so close to killing off Battery D as Captain Harry did today!" groaned one worn-out veteran.

★ ★ ★ ★ ★ ★ **12** ★ ★ ★ ★ ★ ★

Fair Deal and Foul Balls

Franklin D. Roosevelt had called his program to improve American life the New Deal. As he began his new term, President Truman called his program the Fair Deal. He asked Congress to spend more for education, to support civil rights, to build low-income housing. On Capitol Hill he found almost as much opposition as he had confronted in the Republican 80th Congress. Republicans and conservative Democrats blocked most of his bills.

Truman decided there was one thing he could do on his own. Acting as commander-in-chief of the armed forces, he ordered his solicitor general, Charles Fahy, to form a committee to push the nation's military leaders toward implementing the executive order against segregation that he had issued in the summer of 1948. It took over a year of struggling with reluctant generals and admirals, but the president got his way. By the time his second term ended, all three services were committed to training and promoting blacks on a basis of strict equality with whites—and giving qualified blacks the chance to command white men.

While diplomats and cabinet ministers watched, on August 24, 1949, President Truman signed one of the most important documents of his presidency, the North Atlantic Treaty Organization alliance. NATO committed the United States to join the nations of western Europe in mutual defense against Communist aggression. It was the cornerstone of Truman's policy of "containing" communism. (HARRY S TRUMAN LIBRARY)

A much bigger and more public fight erupted in Congress over Mr. Truman's attempt to implement the North Atlantic Treaty Organization to defend Western Europe against Communist aggression. As 1949 began, the Russians had thirty well-armed divisions on the borders of West Germany. The United States and England had five. The other European countries could add a few more, but they had antiquated pre–World War II equipment. To help the allies modernize their armies, the president asked Congress for $1.4 billion.

The uproar was immense. Even Senator Vandenberg, who had helped create NATO, attacked the idea of giving it teeth. He said the treaty of alliance—the piece of paper everyone had signed—was enough to stop Russian aggression. Truman politely disagreed with his old friend—and once more he got his way. The Senate voted the money, 55–24.

In Europe, the president also had to knock heads to make our allies think sensibly. None of them wanted to surrender even a shred of their armies to create a unified force. President Truman persuaded them that this would enable the Russians to conquer them one by one. He resolved their jealousies by appointing Gen. Dwight D. Eisenhower the first commander of NATO—and committing four American divisions to Europe as the backbone of the force.

Republican senator Taft of Ohio declared that Truman did not have the power to send American troops abroad without the consent of Congress. Truman bluntly informed him he was wrong. To prove it, he sent him quotations from a book, *Our Chief Magistrate and His Power,* written by William Howard Taft, the only man who had served both as president and as chief justice of the United States, and who also happened to be Senator Taft's father.

While he was achieving these foreign policy triumphs in Europe, Truman and the United States were suffering a major defeat on the other side of the world. A civil war had been brewing in China between the Communists under Mao Tse-tung and the Nationalists under Chiang Kai-shek. The president had sent General Marshall to try to rescue the situation, but his attempt to reconcile the two sides ended in failure.

The Russians turned over huge amounts of captured Japanese weapons to Mao's men. The United States backed the Nationalists with guns and money. But their government was weak and divided and many generals were corrupt or incompetent. Communist armies soon drove the remnants of Chiang's army to the island of Taiwan, off the Chinese coast, and in the summer of 1949, Mao and his followers took over the government of the largest country in the world.

In the Senate, Republicans rushed to blame Truman for "losing China." They accused him of tolerating Communist sympathizers in the government, who cut off aid to the Nationalists. This was nonsense; but the accusations, repeated day and night, rapidly became a "Big Lie" that many people thought was true.

The political atmosphere was further poisoned by the trial of Alger Hiss. This former State Department official was accused of being a Communist. He denied it under oath before a congressional committee. A former Communist, Whittaker Chambers, produced convincing evidence that Hiss was lying. The government prosecuted Hiss for perjury, and he was found guilty.

Truman's new secretary of state, Dean Acheson, had known Hiss when he was in the State Department. Shocked by his conviction, he declared, "I will not turn my back on Alger Hiss." He explained that he was expressing the sympathy that the Christian gospel urged people to show to prisoners. Numerous senators demanded that Truman fire Acheson. He ignored them—and supplied his critics with more ammunition.

In the midst of these political uproars, a much larger crisis loomed. On September 3, 1949, an air force weather plane on patrol from Japan to Alaska discovered evidence in the atmosphere that the Russians had exploded an atomic bomb. The Atomic Energy Commission panicked and urged Truman to issue an immediate statement. He calmed them down, studied the situation for two weeks, and issued a brief statement aimed at avoiding public hysteria. He reminded the American people that four years earlier he had warned them that the Russians were working on a bomb and that eventually their research would catch up to America's.

Truman was now faced with another momentous decision. Should he authorize the development of an even more powerful bomb, which could be created by splitting the hydrogen atom? Once more, he approached the problem in a calm, methodical way. He appointed a committee of top experts to study the subject and make a report to him.

Unfortunately, one of the senators on the Atomic Energy Commission decided he preferred headlines to clear thinking. He revealed the H-bomb debate on television and accused the chairman, David Lilienthal, of trying to give away U.S. atomic secrets to England and Canada. This put terrific pressure on Truman to make a quick decision—but he resisted it.

Not until January 31, 1950, more than six months after the news of the first Russian explosion reached the White House, did he accept the advice of his committee and order the development of the H-bomb. He signed the order "as part of my responsibility as commander in chief of the armed forces" to make sure the United States could defend itself against any aggressor. He added his firm hope that none of these bombs would ever be used.

But the political furor over the bomb did not go away. From England came dismaying news that a German-born physicist named Klaus Fuchs had given many atomic secrets to the Russians. He was part of a spy ring that had smuggled secrets out of the American factories where the atomic bomb was built during World War II.

Truman immediately saw that this news was going to create a new wave of hysteria over Communists in the American government. He was already deeply concerned about the way some senators, such as Pat McCarran, a Democrat from Nevada, were dealing with the problem. McCarran had persuaded the Senate to give the Defense Department and the State Department the authority to fire anyone suspected of being a Communist without any right of appeal.

As Klaus Fuchs and his American friends, who were soon rounded up by the FBI, demonstrated, Communist sympathizers in the government were not an entirely imaginary threat. Truman set up a loyalty program to dig into the background of anyone suspected of treasonous activities—but he tried to build into it safeguards that gave the accused persons the right to a fair hearing. Conservatives criticized him for being too cautious—and liberals attacked him for raising the whole issue of loyalty.

This set the stage for the appearance of one of the most disreputable politicians of the century, Senator Joseph McCarthy of Wisconsin. On February 9, 1950, six days after the news of Klaus Fuchs's treachery had reached Washington, and nineteen days after Alger Hiss had been found guilty, Senator McCarthy gave a speech in Wheeling, West Virginia. He waved a piece of paper at his audience and told them it was a list of 205 Communist party members in the U.S. State Department.

McCarthy proceeded to fly around the nation repeating these charges. He orated in the Senate about them, frequently changing the numbers, probably because he was drunk. Headlines blossomed. Truman tried to ignore the senator. He was not the first man to make a career out of screaming about Communists in the government. Martin Dies, the head of the House Un-American Activities

Committee, had been at it for years. Truman dismissed McCarthy's charges as a red herring—a trick to divert attention from more important matters.

The president concentrated on formulating a policy that would guide the nation for the duration of the Cold War. He saw that the conflict might last a long time, and he knew that in the government, it was important to have policies spelled out. So he ordered the preparation of a study by the National Security Council. The result was NSC-68—a sweeping survey that drew on the best thinking of the Defense and State departments.

NSC-68 said that the United States and her allies should avoid aggressive actions against the Communists. But they should build up their armed forces so they could pursue a policy of "containment." This meant that they would not tolerate Communist attempts to take over free governments by force. This would require a much stronger army and navy than the United States had in 1949. As was the custom after every war, the United States had disarmed itself into a posture of alarming weakness—and Congress was showing its usual reluctance to vote the money to restore our strength.

President Truman decided to take the case to the country. In the spring of 1950, he embarked on another whistle-stop campaign. He wanted to get the people behind the military buildup—and along the way get in a few good shots at Senator McCarthy. The president was irked at the way supposedly respectable Republican senators, such as Robert Taft, were egging on the swarthy liar from Wisconsin. Taft said that McCarthy should "keep talking and if one case doesn't work out, he should proceed with another."

Again and again, crossing the continent, Truman mocked the Republicans as phony Communist fighters. If they really meant what they were saying, they would stop ranting about a few Communists in the government and vote the money that would make America strong enough "to guarantee a century of peace." This is what Truman saw as the real goal of the policy of containment.

By the time he returned to Washington, the president had spoken to 525,000 Americans—and McCarthy and his friends were reeling. They had no proof of their phony allegations—and no answer when Truman called the senator from Wisconsin "the Kremlin's greatest asset."

Truman was feeling so confident about the way things were going in the country and in the world that he decided to spend a few days in Independence. Before he left, he dedicated a new airport in Baltimore. In his speech, he stressed one of his favorite themes—the importance of planning for the future. "If we had listened to the old mossbacks, we would never have given up the stagecoach," he said. "Some of those old stagecoach mossbacks are still with us—in Congress."

He flew to Kansas City and drove to Independence, where he had a pleasant family dinner with Bess, Margaret, and some friends. As he settled down to read a history book that evening, the telephone rang. It was the secretary of state, Dean Acheson.

"Mr. President," he said. "I have very serious news. The North Koreans have invaded South Korea."

Life in the Truman White House would never be the same.

13

★ ★ ★ ★ ★ ★
★ ★ ★ ★ ★ ★

Truman's Third War

Korea is a small Asian country on a peninsula bordering China. It had been conquered and occupied by Japan in 1894. The Americans and the Russians restored its independence after World War II, but they could not agree on how to unite it. So they divided it into separate countries. North Korea became a typical Communist state, run by a Stalin-like dictator named Kim Il Sung. South Korea became a democracy headed by President Syngman Rhee.

When President Truman received word of the Communist invasion of South Korea, he had good reason to fear that North Korea's attack was the first of many Communist assaults to come. The Russians still vastly outnumbered NATO's armed forces in Europe. Iran and Turkey were being threatened by large Russian armies on their borders. Might the Russians, who had armed the North Koreans, be waiting to see how the Americans responded before launching an attack to seize control of Germany, divided into Communist and democratic states, similar to Korea?

Truman once more demonstrated his amazing ability

to stay calm—and keep the nation calm. On Sunday, June 26, the day after the warning phone call from the secretary of state, he asked Bess and Margaret to go to church, while he drove out to the family farm to visit his younger brother Vivian. They inspected a new milking machine and chatted about local matters. Truman did not mention the situation in Korea to Vivian or anyone else. He wanted everyone to think he had nothing important on his mind, while he waited for more news from Korea.

Back in Independence, aides handed him a grim telegram from the American ambassador to South Korea. "It would appear from the nature of the attack and the manner in which it was launched that it constitutes an all-out offensive against the Republic of Korea."

Even gloomier was a cable from Gen. Douglas MacArthur, the American commander in the Far East. "Enemy effort serious in strength and strategic intent and is undisguised act of war." Worse news came via another telephone call from Secretary of State Dean Acheson, reporting that the North Korean army had deployed over a hundred modern tanks and had made seven amphibious landings along South Korea's coast. Tank-led columns had already advanced to within a few miles of South Korea's capital, Seoul. Acheson thought the United States should immediately ask the United Nations to condemn the invasion. The president agreed.

Truman decided it was time to get back to Washington. He ordered the secretary of state to gather the top officials from the State and Defense departments for a meeting at Blair House, which was still serving as the temporary White House. As he flew to this council of war, Truman remembered what had happened before World War II, when the democracies had allowed the dictators in Japan and Germany to swallow up country after country.

Truman vowed that he was not going to let that happen. When he landed in Washington, he was delighted to learn that the United Nations, moving with a speed that caught Soviet Russia off guard, had passed a stinging resolution, denouncing North Korea's "unprovoked act of aggression."

By eight o'clock on June 26, Truman was in Blair House meeting with his top advisers. After discussing the situation in detail, he ordered General MacArthur to supply the South Korean army with all available weapons and ammunition. He also ordered the Seventh Fleet into Formosa Strait, between Taiwan and the mainland, to make sure Chinese Communists did not try to seize the island.

The president then went around the room and asked every man what he thought the United States should do. There was, he said later, "no suggestion from anyone that either the United States or the United Nations should back away from this aggression." The big question was whether to commit ground troops. Some people thought—or hoped—that air and naval support would be enough. But Gen. Omar Bradley, chairman of the Joint Chiefs of Staff, grimly disagreed. The South Korean Army had no tanks and no artillery. The United States had given them only light weapons to maintain order in their own country.

Knowing he could not go to war against North Korea without the approval of Congress, Truman met with fifteen leading senators and congressmen. He read them a statement he was planning to issue, declaring that the United States intended to support South Korea. They asked if the nations of Western Europe would support the American initiative.

Secretary of State Acheson waved telegrams from London, Paris, Rome, and other capitals, confirming Europe's backing. Truman ordered the commander of the air force to give the senators and congressmen top-secret information about our air strength in the Far East. Finally, Sen. Tom Connally of Texas said, "This is the clearest test the United Nations has ever faced."

Truman now had congressional support to release his statement. It instantly became one of the turning points of American history. Joseph C. Harsch of the *Christian Science Monitor* said that never in his twenty years in Washington had he felt "such a sense of relief and unity pass through the city." The *New York Times* said it produced "a transformation of the American government." From South Korea, Ambassador John Muccio reported that without the statement, the government would have collapsed and surrendered.

But words do not win wars. The news from the fighting front continued to be very bad. South Korea's army had already suffered 50 percent casualties. Earlier in the week, Truman had asked the Russians to pressure North Korea into withdrawing. Moscow now replied with a cold refusal, backed by blatant lies. They claimed to have nothing to do with the attack, and piously protested that they would never dream of interfering in Korea's internal affairs.

Even more dismaying was a report the president received from a diplomat who had just returned from Tokyo. When the North Koreans attacked, General MacArthur had been nowhere to be found and none of his aides had dared to interrupt his off-duty hours. The diplomat urged Truman to replace him with a younger, more vigorous general. The president sidestepped this problem for the time being. Famous for his exploits in World War I and World War II, MacArthur had too many friends in Congress to be fired without very strong reasons.

The next day, MacArthur, now very much on the job, flew to Korea to make a personal inspection of the battlefront. When he saw the chaos in the South Korean army, he cabled President Truman for permission to commit a regimental combat team of American infantry. There was no other hope of stopping the North Koreans. "Time is of the essence," MacArthur warned.

Six days after he heard the bad news from Secretary of State Acheson in Independence, Truman was faced with one of the most agonizing decisions of his presidency. He had lived through two wars and fought in one of them. He knew what war meant in terms of blood and death and sacrifice. Yet he could not back away from the decision if his previous words of support to South Korea were to have any meaning.

Once more Truman summoned the congressional leaders—eighteen this time. He told them he was sending in the infantry. The Republicans immediately attacked him for making the decision without a vote of Congress. Truman insisted this situation was different from other wars in American history—they were now fighting under the banner of the United Nations. It was a "police action," designed to suppress North Korean "bandits."

Truman reiterated his intention to consult Congress. But he resisted the Republican contention that he had to get congressional approval to use troops in such a situation. He considered this a serious dilution of the powers of the presidency. He ordered the State Department to prepare a memorandum that listed eighty-seven instances since the founding of the nation when the president as commander in chief had ordered the army or the navy into action without congressional approval. In a world of jet aircraft and surprise attacks, Truman believed America could not survive if the president lacked this power.

General MacArthur committed American infantry from

the occupation forces in Japan. To everyone's dismay, the tank-backed North Koreans mauled these unprepared troops almost as badly as they had shattered the South Korean army. The Americans were soon driven to the south end of the peninsula, where they clung to a small bridgehead around the port of Pusan.

With Americans dying from Communist gunfire in Korea, the demagogues in the Senate renewed their screams about Communists in the government. Sen. Pat McCarran, in consultation with Sen. Joseph McCarthy and others, introduced a bill that set up a Subversive Activities Control Board with sweeping powers to hunt down suspected traitors. Truman called it a "thought control" bill and vetoed it. The Senate passed it over his veto—a crushing defeat.

From Japan, General MacArthur renewed a suggestion he had already made—to use the troops of Chiang Kai-shek, on Taiwan. Chiang was eager to commit his men against a Communist foe—obviously hoping that the Chinese Communists would join the war and, with the United States for an ally, he would regain control of China. Truman had turned down the idea once. He was trying not to let the war spread beyond Korea. He turned it down again.

On July 31, without any authorization from the president, MacArthur flew to Taiwan to confer with Chiang. The Chinese leader offered MacArthur command of all his troops. MacArthur rejected the offer—but Chiang announced to an excited world that MacArthur favored an attack on mainland China by his soldiers.

Truman sent one of his top advisers, Ambassador Averell Harriman, to Japan to warn MacArthur against making his own foreign policy. MacArthur claimed it was all a misunderstanding. But a month later, he issued a

Truman meets General Douglas MacArthur on Wake Island in the mid-Pacific to discuss the future of the Korean War. It was the first time the two men had ever met. MacArthur vowed to make no more political statements—a promise he soon broke. (U.S. ARMY, COURTESY HARRY S TRUMAN LIBRARY)

statement to the Veterans of Foreign Wars, which declared that the president's policy to keep Taiwan neutral was a mistake.

At that point, Truman seriously considered firing General MacArthur. But he decided against it because MacArthur had produced a daring plan to reverse the deteriorating military situation in Korea.

MacArthur proposed to make an end run on the North Korean army, which was concentrated at the south end of the peninsula, attacking the Americans around Pusan. He wanted to land two divisions at Inchon on the west coast of Korea, close to the waist of the peninsula. They would drive inland and cut the Communists' supply lines, trapping them between two American forces.

The Joint Chiefs of Staff were leery of the idea. The Inchon invasion force would have only a few hours to land and secure a bridgehead before the tide went out and their ships would be mired in two miles of mud flats. President Truman called it "a bold plan worthy of a master strategist," and backed the daring gamble with the full authority of his office.

On September 15, 1950, MacArthur's men stormed ashore at Inchon, totally surprising the North Koreans. Simultaneously the men in the Pusan perimeter went over to the attack. The North Korean army dissolved into panicky fragments. Over 130,000 surrendered. By September 29, the Americans and South Koreans had regained Seoul and South Korea was a free country again.

Typically, President Truman did not take any credit for Inchon. Instead he showered praise on General MacArthur. "Few operations in military history can match the brilliant maneuver which has now resulted in the liberation of Seoul," he said in a telegram to the general.

MacArthur deserved the praise, but Truman would regret those words before another year went by.

14

Bullets and Ballots

President Truman—and the United Nations—were now faced with a grave decision. They had kicked the North Koreans out of South Korea. Could they now reunite the country? With enthusiastic backing from the UN, Truman decided to give it a try. He ordered General MacArthur to pursue and destroy what was left of the North Korean army, hoping the Communist regime would collapse without the support of its bayonets.

Ominous noises came from Red China. Its state radio declared it would send troops into North Korea if MacArthur's soldiers crossed the border at the 38th parallel. Truman conveyed this warning to MacArthur, who dismissed it as an attempt to scare North Koreans away from voting for a free and united country. Nevertheless, Truman remained nervous about this threat and decided it was time to confer face-to-face with MacArthur. Since the end of World War II, the general had remained in Japan overseeing that nation's transition to democracy.

The general and the president met for the first time in their lives on October 15, 1950, at Wake Island in the center of the Pacific Ocean. The general was very friendly and respectful to the president. He apologized for his statement to the Veterans of Foreign Wars, criticizing Truman's policy of keeping Taiwan neutral. He said Republican politicians had made him a "chump" by maneuvering him into disagreeing with the president.

Truman asked him what he thought of the chances for Chinese or Russian interference in Korea.

"Very little," MacArthur said. He felt there was nothing to worry about even if the Chinese did come in. The UN army could easily handle them. The general did not think the Chinese would risk more than fifty or sixty thousand men on such an adventure. Moreover, he claimed, they had no air force worth mentioning, giving the UN complete control of the air.

They discussed how much longer the war would last. "I hope to get the Eighth Army home by Christmas," MacArthur said.

Truman flew back to the United States in a hopeful mood. He made a speech in San Francisco calling on the Soviet Union and other Communist nations to join him in upholding the United Nations charter. "The only victory we seek [in Korea] is the victory of peace," he said.

In North Korea, the UN army, which consisted of the American Eighth Army and the revived South Korean army, began the drive north. Almost immediately, worrisome things began to happen. On October 26, they captured a Chinese soldier. On October 30, they captured more Chinese soldiers. The following day an American regiment was attacked by masses of howling Chinese troops after being bombarded by mortar and rocket fire. Heavily outnumbered, the regiment collapsed and the survivors fled into the hills.

That same day in Washington Truman discovered he,

President Truman greets General Dwight Eisenhower in early 1951 when he returned from Europe to report on the North Atlantic Treaty Organization (NATO). Truman appointed Eisenhower to this vital post to reassure European allies of U.S. commitment to support them against Soviet aggression. (NATIONAL PARK SERVICE, ABBIE ROWE, COURTESY HARRY S TRUMAN LIBRARY)

too, could become the target of flying bullets. Two members of Puerto Rico's tiny Independence Party, who thought violence would help their cause, tried to assassinate the president.

One, Gisel Torresola, approached Blair House from the west. The other man, Oscar Collazo, approached from the east. The entrance to the house, which was up a few steps from the sidewalk, was guarded by White House policemen in booths. The assassins planned to kill the guards and rush into the house to shoot the president.

Collazo opened fire first, hitting Private Donald T. Birdzell in the leg. Birdzell staggered into the street, drawing his gun. Collazo charged up the steps toward the front door, which was wide open. But the guards in the east booth cut him down with a blast of gunfire.

A moment later, the second gunman, Torresola, opened fire on the east booth guards, mortally wounding Private Leslie Coffelt. Frightened by the fate of his partner, this second assassin did not try to charge the door.

The president was upstairs getting ready to attend the dedication of a statue to a World War II British general. Startled by the gunfire, Mrs. Truman looked out the window and saw Private Birdzell and Coffelt bleeding in the street. "Harry!" she cried. "Someone's shooting our policemen!"

Concerned only for her safety, Truman drew her back and peered out the window while shots were still being exchanged with Torresola. The dying Private Coffelt got off one more shot, killing Torresola instantly with a bullet in the head.

Moments later, the street was full of Secret Service agents. "Get back, get back!" they implored the president, fearing that there might be more gunmen waiting to open fire on him. In three chaotic minutes, no fewer than 27 shots had already been fired.

Unruffled as always, Truman insisted on going through with the dedication ceremony. "A president has to expect those things," he said.

In Korea, the military bulletins grew ominous. More and more American units reported violent encounters with Chinese soldiers. On November 6, the day before the midterm congressional elections, General MacArthur abruptly broadcast to the whole world a request for permission to bomb the bridges over the Yalu River, which separated Korea from China.

Truman, still hoping the war would not spread, gave him permission to destroy only the Korean end of these bridges. A few days later, MacArthur demanded the right to pursue Chinese Communist planes across the river to their "sanctuaries." It was a strange request from a general who had told the president that the Chinese had no air force. Truman turned him down—although he knew that to some voters, this made him seem "soft on communism," Senator McCarthy's favorite smear.

Although MacArthur claimed he had severed his ties with the Republican party's leaders, he was obviously still working closely with them. They dangled in front of him the possibility that he might be their nominee for president in 1952, and the general could not resist the lure. MacArthur's maneuvers, combined with McCarthy's continued smear campaign, hurt the Democrats badly in the midterm elections.

Three of the Senate's leading Democrats went down to defeat. Most dismaying to Truman was the loss of Sen. Millard Tydings of Maryland, who had been an outspoken foe of Senator McCarthy. The unscrupulous demagogue had circulated fake pictures, supposedly showing Tydings with Earl Browder, the head of the American Communist party, suggesting that the senator was his willing tool. Truman would miss Tydings's support.

In Korea, the situation continued to slide toward disaster. MacArthur chose to ignore the warnings of Communist intervention. He divided his army into two columns, making it more vulnerable to attack, and launched a "home by Christmas" drive toward the Chinese border. On November 26, both columns were attacked by over 300,000 Chinese Communist troops and driven back in headlong retreat.

In Washington, President Truman reported the news to his stunned staff in a calm, quiet voice. "The Chinese have come in with both feet," he said. "This is the worst situation we've had yet. We'll just have to meet it as we've met all the rest."

With crisp authority, the president ordered the preparation of a declaration of national emergency. Then he placed the blame where he thought it belonged: on Senator McCarthy and his friends. "The liars have accomplished their purpose," he said. He pointed to a recent article in the Russian newspaper *Pravda,* crowing about the bitter quarrels in the American government. The Chinese thought they were attacking a weak, divided country.

In Korea, MacArthur began to panic. "This small command is facing the entire Chinese nation in an undeclared war," he said. "Unless some immediate action is taken, hope for success cannot be justified." He was again demanding the right to attack Chinese bases in Manchuria — a move that might have ignited another world war. He was acting like the commander of a collapsing army. He seemed unaware that his soldiers had made a fighting retreat, losing about 13,000 dead and wounded, but remaining a strong, well-equipped force of over 250,000 men.

Back in the United States, reporters created another panic. In the course of a press conference, one of them asked if Truman might use the atomic bomb in Korea. "There has always been active consideration of its use," the president said. "It is a terrible weapon and should not be used on innocent men, women, and children who have nothing whatsoever to do with this aggression."

Ignoring these last remarks, the newsmen wrote sensational headlines implying that the bomb was about to be used. Papers in Europe embroidered the story, reporting that planes loaded with atom bombs were on the runways in Japan, ready to take off. An appalled Charlie Ross, working overtime as the president's press secretary, tried to straighten things out, but the damage had been done. In England, Prime Minister Clement Atlee announced that he was going to fly to Washington to "restrain" Truman.

Not wanting to cause any more international tension, the president welcomed Atlee and arranged for a series of meetings to discuss the world's problems. This put even heavier pressure on Charlie Ross, who had twice as many reporters swarming around the White House now, asking him what the two leaders were discussing.

On December 5, the second day of Atlee's visit, Ross worked all day and returned to the White House that night for another briefing. Some TV newsmen asked him to go on camera for a statement for the evening news. As Charlie rose to speak, he toppled back into his chair, his face ashen. His secretary called the White House doctor. He was there in minutes, but it was too late. Charlie Ross was dead.

President Truman returned from a conference with Atlee on the presidential yacht *Williamsburg* and was told the news. With tears in his eyes, he sat at his desk and wrote out a long tribute to Charlie. "The friend of my youth," it began, "who became a tower of strength when the responsibilities of high office so unexpectedly fell to me, is gone."

When Harry Truman tried to read the statement to the reporters, his voice broke. He could not finish it. "Ah, hell," he said, handing it to one of them. "I can't read this thing. You fellows know how I feel, anyway."

15

The President Blows a Fuse

December 5, 1950, was unquestionably one of the worst days in Harry Truman's life. His hopes of a victorious peace in Korea had evaporated. He had lost one of his closest friends, Charlie Ross—a man who had kept working at his demanding job out of loyalty to Truman, even though he had been warned that his heart was bad.

That night, instead of being able to withdraw to regain his balance, Truman had to make a public appearance on behalf of his daughter, Margaret. Her singing career had continued to prosper. Tonight she was appearing for the first time in Washington, D.C., at Constitution Hall, one of the nation's premier showcases for performing artists.

Truman ordered his staff not to mention Charlie Ross's death to Margaret. He was afraid it would affect her performance. Margaret usually spent most of the day in seclusion before she sang, so this was easy to do. Later, Margaret, who was very close to Charlie, said, "I think I should have been told that my friend had died."

From the beginning of her performance, Margaret sensed that the atmosphere in Constitution Hall was charged "not only with grief but with mystery." Something was wrong with the audience's reaction, and she did not know what it was. Nevertheless, she did not think it affected her singing. At intermission, the music critic from the Washington *Times-Herald* came backstage to congratulate her.

Truman naturally enjoyed the performance. He adored his daughter. He also admired the accompanist, who, after intermission, played two solo pieces, one a Truman favorite, the Chopin Waltz in A-Flat, opus 42. "He did it as well as it could be done and I've heard Paderewski, Rosenthal, and Josef Lhevinne play it," the president later wrote.

The next morning, Truman awoke at 6 A.M. as usual and took his half-hour walk at 120 paces a minute, reporters puffing in his wake. Back at Blair House he opened the Washington *Post* and read a horrendous review of Margaret's performance by the paper's music critic, Paul Hume. "She is flat a good deal of the time," he wrote. "She cannot sing with anything approaching professional polish. She communicates almost nothing of the music she presents."

Not satisfied with demolishing Margaret, Hume proceeded to attack the accompanist as well. "The only thing he didn't criticize," said Gen. George Marshall, who was one of Margaret's most devoted fans, "was the varnish on the piano."

Again and again, Harry Truman had demonstrated an almost superhuman ability to stay calm in a crisis. But this time, he blew a fuse. Without telling a soul, including Margaret or Bess, he wrote Hume a letter on White House stationery.

> I have just read your lousy review buried in the back pages. You sound like a frustrated man that never made a success, an eight-ulcer man on a four-ulcer job with all four ulcers working.

I have never met you, but if I do you'll need a new nose and plenty of beefsteak and perhaps a supporter below. Westbrook Pegler,* a guttersnipe, is a gentleman compared to you. You can take that as more of an insult than a reflection on your ancestry.

Truman sealed and stamped the letter, summoned one of his favorite White House servants, and asked him to mail it. Two days later, the Washington *Post* published it and the uproar was intense. Dozens of newspapers ran editorials complaining that Truman was not a gentleman. His aides feared that he had damaged his image as president.

"Wait till the mail comes in," Truman said. "I'll make you a bet that eighty percent of it is on my side."

A week later, Truman marched his staff to the White House mail room. Thousands of letters about his blast at Hume had poured in from across the country and were piled in stacks along the walls. The mail room staff had kept careful count of the opinions. Just over 80 percent had supported the president. Most were from mothers and fathers who thought he had a perfect right to defend his daughter.

"The trouble with you guys is, you just don't understand human nature," Truman said as he led the staff back to the business of dealing with the crisis in Korea.

*A Hearst newspaper reporter noted for his violent language.

16

The President Fires
a General

The situation in Korea deteriorated daily as the Chinese Communists threw in more and more troops. They attacked the UN army in gigantic waves, indifferent to casualties. The South Koreans could not stand against them for more than five minutes. Again and again the Americans had to plug huge holes in their defense line when an entire Korean division fled into the hills. MacArthur's men had to give ground, abandoning Seoul, the Korean capital.

Panic swirled through Washington. The Joint Chiefs of Staff warned the president that the UN army might have to evacuate the peninsula. Prime Minister Atlee wanted to cut a deal with the Chinese to get a quick peace. The United Nations declined to condemn Chinese aggression in Korea, apparently because they feared it might offend them.

In the Senate, twenty-four Republicans endorsed a resolution accusing Truman of making secret commitments to Atlee. In the House, Republicans demanded the resignation of Secretary of State Acheson, claiming—once more—he was "soft on communism."

Joseph P. Kennedy, father of future president John F. Kennedy, called for the immediate withdrawal of American forces from Korea, Berlin, and Europe. He said American policy was "morally bankrupt." Ex-President Herbert Hoover advised an immediate retreat of all our soldiers, everywhere, to American shores. Otherwise western civilization was doomed.

Truman ignored this panicky advice. "We did not get into this fight with the idea of being licked," he said. "We cannot desert our friends when the going gets rough."

In Korea, a brilliant American soldier began putting teeth into the president's words. Gen. Matthew Ridgway took command of the UN army on December 25, replacing Gen. Walton Walker, who had been killed in a jeep accident. General MacArthur remained the overall commander in the Far East, operating from his headquarters in Tokyo.

Wearing hand grenades on a belt across his chest, Ridgway traveled by land and by air up and down the cold, snowy defense line, visiting every division in his army. He dismissed defeatist generals and spread a message of courage and resolution to his troops. There were not going to be any more retreats, he said. As soon as possible, the UN army was going over to the attack.

In New York, the UN offered Communist China admission to the UN and control—the surrender, actually—of Taiwan, if China agreed to an immediate truce in Korea. The United States fought the idea, but lost the vote. To Truman's relief, the Chinese overplayed their hand. They announced they would take the UN's offer—but insisted on the right to keep fighting until their army destroyed the capitalist aggressors in Korea.

Just as the Chinese Communist leaders were flaunting their arrogance in Beijing, their army in Korea found itself in deep trouble. Their much heralded third and final offensive petered out with horrendous casualties. General Ridgway ordered the UN army to attack on January 25. Suddenly UN members showed amazing political courage. They rejected the Chinese counteroffer and branded the Communist regime an aggressor.

The turnaround pleased President Truman, but his pleasure was overshadowed by complaints from his Far Eastern commander. Instead of praising General Ridgway and his men, MacArthur groused that Korea had become an "accordion war" that America could not win. Each side would advance until its supply line got too long and then be forced to retreat. In a public statement he demanded an air and sea blockade of the Chinese coast, bombing raids on Chinese cities, and the use of Chiang Kai-shek's forces in Korea.

MacArthur made this statement just as President Truman was planning to issue a call to Red China for a cease-fire, to be followed by negotiations to settle the conflict in Korea. The Joint Chiefs of Staff had informed MacArthur of the president's intentions. A wise general would have kept quiet and waited for Truman to speak.

Instead, MacArthur issued his own peace proposal. He began by scoffing at the Red Chinese army and boasting that he had cleared them out of South Korea. Finally he demanded that the Chinese come to the peace table—and threatened them with an all-out attack if they did not respond. It was hardly the way to persuade a militant, revolutionary regime to talk peace. The Chinese angrily rejected MacArthur's proposal. The Far Eastern commander was clearly out of control.

President Truman was furious. "I was ready to kick

MacArthur into the North China sea," he said later. "I was never so put out in my life." But the president remained outwardly calm. He was fighting for congressional approval of appropriations and troop commitments for NATO and he did not want to endanger these bills, so vital to the security of Europe. So he let MacArthur off with a sharp reprimand from the Joint Chiefs of Staff, ordering him to make no more political statements of any kind.

MacArthur promised to obey, and the truce between the president and the general lasted a few more weeks. But on April 5, the Republican minority leader of the House of Representatives, Joseph Martin, read a letter to his fellow congressmen from the general. Martin had sent MacArthur a speech he had made, attacking Truman's foreign policy, and asked him to comment on it.

MacArthur's letter claimed that his views on how to fight the war had been ignored in Washington. He said it was "strangely difficult" for some people to realize that in Asia they were fighting communism for control of the globe. "As you point out, we must win. There is no substitute for victory," he wrote.

That day, President Truman jotted some thoughts on his White House calendar.

MacArthur shoots another political bomb through Joe Martin . . .
This looks like the last straw.
Rank insubordination. I call in Gen. Marshall, Dean Acheson, Averell Harriman and General Bradley and they come to the conclusion that our Big General in the Far East must be recalled.

Gen. MacArthur was about to join the long list of those who learned the hard way that no one pushed Harry Truman around.

That night Gen. Marshall, who had returned to Truman's cabinet as secretary of defense, read the file on MacArthur and concluded that he should have been fired two years before. The president called in the congressional leaders of the Democratic party and told them what he was going to do. On April 9, Truman ordered a message of dismissal sent to the general. He also issued a statement saying that he had made the decision "with deep regret" because the general was "unable to give his wholehearted support to the policies of the United States government and the United Nations."

The next day, the president jotted the public reaction on his desk calender in his usual calm, matter-of-fact way: "Quite an explosion. Was expected, but I had to act. Telegrams and letters of abuse by the dozen."

MacArthur returned to a hysterical welcome in San Francisco and other cities. Dozens of people, including several senators, called for Truman's impeachment. Senator McCarthy said Truman had fired MacArthur while drunk. The general addressed a joint session of Congress and the Corps of Cadets at West Point. A Gallup Poll reported 62 percent of the population backed the general. A foreigner would have wondered if the United States was on the brink of a military coup d'état.

But President Truman was confident that once the American people calmed down, the majority would decide he was right. This was exactly what happened. The Senate voted to hold hearings on the general's dismissal. Many important people testified.

MacArthur had claimed his fellow generals on the Joint Chiefs of Staff agreed with him but were "muzzled" by the president. There was no sign of a muzzle on Gen. Omar Bradley when he told the Senate that MacArthur's policy was just plain wrong. It would have involved us "in the wrong war, at the wrong place, at the wrong time and with the wrong enemy."

Other generals severely criticized MacArthur's strategy and tactics in his "home by Christmas" offensive. When the Senate asked the general to explain how his policy would have produced a victory, his comments were vague and confusing. He admitted it would have been foolish to invade China and start a war with its 400 million people. Pretty soon most people realized the general was full of hot air.

In his memoirs, Gen. Matthew Ridgway, the man who replaced MacArthur as the Far Eastern commander, wrote that "it was a boon to the country" that President Truman had acted to protect his constitutional power as commander in chief of the armed forces of the United States. General Ridgway thought Truman's decision would be a powerful safeguard in a future crisis if a popular general tried to challenge the authority of a president.

★ ★ ★ ★ ★ ★ **17** ★ ★ ★ ★ ★ ★

A President Embattled

The war went on in Korea. The Chinese army continued to suffer heavy casualties as American planes hammered their front line troops and supply lines. Typhus and other diseases added to their death toll. Meanwhile, other nations—Great Britain, Turkey, Canada—sent soldiers to bolster the ranks of the UN army, though most of the troops remained American. GI's continued to die from Communist bullets—giving more ammunition back home to smear specialists like Senator McCarthy.

In mid-June, McCarthy delivered a lengthy speech accusing Gen. Marshall, of all people, of being a Communist. It was a new low point for the senator from Wisconsin. When reporters asked Truman about it, he called it "one of the silliest things I ever heard." George Marshall was Harry Truman's favorite living American. The general had devoted his entire life to the service of his country. His planning and leadership had been crucial to victory in World War II.

Nine days after McCarthy's vicious attack on the president's secretary of defense, the Russian delegate to the United Nations announced that it was time for peace talks in Korea. Three days later, a Chinese spokesman said the same thing. The president ordered General Ridgway to send negotiators to meet with Communist officers and discuss an armistice and cease-fire. But the Communists refused to stop fighting while they talked.

This made Truman the target of continued Republican attacks. The president used his knowledge of history to survive the ordeal. He told one of his friends that there were at least 176 instances of a president making controversial decisions for which he had been savagely criticized. He cited Jefferson's war with the Barbary pirates in the Mediterranean and Lincoln's call for 75,000 volunteers to suppress secession. "It is the business of presidents to meet situations as they arise and to meet them in the public interest," Truman said. He took comfort in noting that no one remembered the attackers.

Gradually the Korean peace negotiators began to make progress. The Communists realized they could not get anywhere by shouting insults and threats. They grudgingly accepted General Ridgway's insistence on drawing a new border between North and South Korea, giving the UN army high ground that was easier to defend. Finally there was only one question to resolve: the prisoners.

The UN army had captured 132,000 North Koreans and Chinese. About half of them had announced that they did not like living under communism and did not want to return. The Communists insisted they all had to return. It was a very tough decision for President Truman to make. He could have had peace early in 1952—if he had been willing to send these men back to life in a Communist dictatorship.

Truman refused. By declaring their wish to stay in the free world, the prisoners had exposed themselves to severe punishment, probably death, if they were forcibly returned. "We will not buy an armistice by turning over human beings to slaughter or slavery," Truman said.

At home, the president faced another crisis. The steel companies and their union could not agree on a new contract. With the troops in Korea dependent on steel to supply them with guns, ammunition, tanks, and planes, Truman announced that he would not tolerate a strike. He ordered a fact-finding study, which revealed that the companies could easily afford the wage hike the workers were asking. But the companies ignored the study and the president's gruff criticism of their stance.

Truman spent hours trying to mediate the dispute, but the companies simply refused to bargain. On April 7, 1952, the union called a strike. Ninety minutes before the walkout began, the president went on the radio to announce that he was seizing ninety-two steel mills to make sure they stayed open to sustain the war effort. "I have to think about our soldiers in Korea," he said.

Congress and the newspapers howled, claiming Truman could not take control of private property without congressional approval. The president sent a message to Capitol Hill, requesting a law that would authorize the seizure in the national interest. Congress declined to pass it. At a press conference, Truman angrily insisted that he had the power to act without them in a national emergency. Again he cited the actions of many earlier presidents to prove his point.

A reporter asked the president if he thought he had the power to seize the nation's radio and television stations. Thoroughly enraged, Truman said, "The president has to act for whatever is for the best interests of the country." Newspapers across the nation rushed to call him a potential dictator—surely the silliest of many charges made against Harry Truman.

A few days later, a federal judge ruled the seizure of the steel mills unconstitutional. The president appealed the case to the Supreme Court—and lost. The steel companies regained their mills and the union promptly went out on strike for seven weeks, which cost the owners $40 million. They finally granted the wage increase—but insisted on Truman permitting them a hefty price increase per ton to pay for it.

All in all, the steel strike was not one of Truman's finer hours. He revealed, in his uncharacteristic remark about seizing the radio and TV stations (which he later called "hooey"), that the White House pressure cooker was taking its toll. He was in the final year of his presidency. It was time to start thinking of his successor.

A few weeks after he was reelected, Truman's old friend, Gen. Harry Vaughan, asked him if he planned to run for another term. "Are you crazy?" the president said.

On November 19, 1951, Truman read a memorandum to his staff stating bluntly that he was not a candidate for reelection to the presidency. He reviewed his long career in politics and said that he favored a two-term limitation for presidents. "In my opinion, eight years as president is enough and sometimes too much for any man to serve in that capacity."

The Republicans and southern conservatives, angry at Franklin Roosevelt for getting elected four times, had already passed a constitutional amendment limiting the presidency to two terms. But Truman had been specifically exempted from its provisions. Moreover, "by a quibble," Truman noted in his memorandum, he could claim that he had not served a full first term—he had been president for forty-five months, instead of forty-eight. But that was not Truman's style. He was determined to uphold the spirit of the two-term precedent.

"There is a lure in power," he wrote in his memorandum. "It can get into a man's blood just as gambling and lust for money have been known to do. This is a republic, the greatest in the world. I want this country to continue as a republic."

During the next six months, Truman and his aides began searching for a successor. There were no obvious candidates. But Truman was not particularly worried because the leading contender for the Republican nomination was the colorless senator from Ohio, Robert Taft.

Suddenly a political earthquake occurred in Europe. Gen. Dwight D. Eisenhower, head of NATO, announced in January 1952 that he was ready to accept a call to higher duties—as a Republican. General "Ike" retained a tremendous popularity with the men he had commanded during World War II—and with the American public. The search for a Democratic opponent suddenly became urgent.

Truman and his aides finally decided their man was Adlai Stevenson, the governor of Illinois. While Truman had carried the state by a squeaky 34,000 votes in 1948, Stevenson had rolled up a majority of 572,000. One of his grandfathers had served as Grover Cleveland's vice president and another had been a leading figure in Abraham Lincoln's administration. Truman thought he had "the background and what it takes" to do the job.

Adlai Stevenson came to the White House at the president's request—talked with Truman for two hours—and left the impression that he was a little reluctant, but he agreed to run. A few days later, Truman discovered that

Stevenson was telling his friends that he had said no. This was a warning of trouble to come.

Truman summoned Stevenson for another meeting. The governor danced away but confirmed to one of Truman's aides that he had said no. That left the Democrats without a candidate. For a few weeks, Truman debated running again. But Bess Truman issued a virtual edict, warning him that if he was reelected, he would find himself without a first lady in the White House. His top aides also advised the president against it.

At General Eidsenhower's request, Truman accepted his resignation as head of NATO. Ike then resigned from the army and began campaigning for the Republican nomination, with Senator Taft as his vigorous opponent. Truman's final conversation with Ike was not very friendly. Ike told him he thought the answer to the world's problems was not a program like Truman's Point Four, which brought new technology to backward nations, but birth control, to limit population growth.

"Do me a favor," Truman said, showing his political instincts. "Make a speech on that topic in Boston, New York, and Chicago." These were strongholds of the Catholic Church, where a candidate would commit political suicide if he took such a position. The general obviously had a lot to learn about politics.

Ike won the Republican nomination, making the choice of a Democratic candidate all the more crucial. Truman badly wanted the Democrats to win the election to vindicate the past four years of his presidency. Three days before the Democratic Convention was to begin, he got a call from Adlai Stevenson, informing him that he was a candidate for the nomination after all.

Truman was speechless. They had wasted six months in which the president could have put all the power and influence of the Democratic party behind Stevenson to give him national stature. Now he was trying to run as a dark-horse candidate. Why?

Stevenson had his own strategy—and it was not flattering to Truman. He wanted to put some distance between himself and the Truman administration. The continuing war in Korea, the steel mill brawl, and an outbreak of corruption in several areas of the administration, such as the Internal Revenue Service, had convinced Stevenson that Truman's support was more a liability than an asset.

Truman did not take long to figure this out. Nevertheless, his loyalty to the Democratic party enabled him to swallow his hurt feelings and support Stevenson because he still thought he was the best man for the job. Truman's backing turned out to be crucial at the Democratic Convention. When Stevenson found himself deadlocked with three other candidates, Truman took charge, ordered one of them to switch his support to the governor—and put him over the top.

The president stood beside the reluctant candidate on the convention platform and declared: "You have nominated a winner, and I am going to take off my coat and do everything I can to help him win."

18

Hail and Farewell

Setting aside his doubts about Adlai Stevenson, Truman did everything in his power to get him elected. But it was a lost cause, almost from the start. Stevenson declined to run on the record of the Truman administration. He ignored its great achievements—the Marshall Plan, the creation of NATO, the rescue of Europe from communism, the policy of containment, the courageous defense of freedom in Korea. He seemed intimidated by the Republican cry that the Democrats had been in the White House too long—and by a Gallup Poll that indicated Truman's popularity rating had sunk to 23 percent.

At one point, Stevenson foolishly agreed with a reporter who wanted to know if he was going to clean up the mess in Washington—another Republican slogan. Truman was even more appalled when Stevenson sounded apologetic about Communists in the government. Truman said he was indirectly endorsing "the most brazen lie of the century"—that the Democrats were soft on communism.

Margaret Truman later said that Stevenson's campaign

made her father "more sad than mad." Eisenhower's campaign enraged him. He was particularly appalled to see Ike appear on the same platform with Republican senator William Jenner of Indiana, who was an imitator of Senator McCarthy. Jenner had called General Marshall a traitor.

Later, General Eisenhower deleted a paragraph praising General Marshall from a speech because Senator McCarthy was also speaking on the same program. Truman could not understand how Ike could be so disloyal to a man who had chosen him as supreme commander in Europe during World War II. "You don't kick the man who made you," Truman said.

Only when Eisenhower had built up a commanding lead in the polls did Stevenson ask the president for help. Truman immediately launched a whistle-stop campaign— and had a very good time hurling adjectives and accusations at the Republicans. He said Ike had fallen into the hands of the "snollygosters." Reporters rushed to their dictionaries and discovered a snollygoster was a clever liar.

As the campaign roared to a climax, Eisenhower decided to ensure his victory by blaming the Democrats for the war in Korea. If elected, he announced he would "go to Korea and put an end to the fighting."

Infuriated, Truman shot back. "Any man who talks like a superman is a fraud."

Eisenhower's assertion made little sense—but it was shrewd politics. The American people were thoroughly sick of the stalemated war. The general buried Adlai Stevenson by six million votes. Truman, still steaming over Ike's fraudulent claim to knowing how to end the war, immediately wired him, declaring his official presidential plane, *Independence,* was available and ready to fly him to Korea.

Ike made the trip and solved nothing. The war was eventually settled on Truman's terms in the summer of 1953. The prisoners who did not want to return to communism became free men.

In spite of his disgust with Eisenhower's campaign, President Truman did his best to make the transition to a Republican administration as smooth as possible. He invited the president-elect to the White House for several briefings on the world situation, and cooperated with aides that Eisenhower appointed to work with the Truman staff.

As he prepared to leave the White House, Truman grew philosophical. He noted that his mail had fallen below 5,000 letters a week for the first time since he took office. "It's fortunate that I've never taken an attitude that the kudos and kow-tows are made to me as an individual. I knew always that the greatest office in the history of the world was getting them, and Harry S Truman as an individual was not. I hope I'm still the country man from Missouri."

One thing that gave Truman great pleasure was a farewell luncheon that the newspaperwomen gave for Mrs. Truman. One of them read a poem in honor of her, which revealed what a good politician she was in her quiet way. The poem opened by declaring that for them, Bess would always be "far more than a figure in history."

> We will think of you rather as a friend
> Whose kindnesses never seemed to end
> The appreciative little longhand note
> For something nice that somebody wrote
> Or the flowers when somebody was sad or ill
> With a card that is surely treasured still.

During his last days in office, Truman had a distinguished visitor, his old friend, Winston Churchill, who had been reelected prime minister in England. One night at dinner, Churchill confessed that when Harry Truman succeeded President Roosevelt, he had misjudged him badly. "Since that time, you, more than any other man, have saved western civilization," Churchill said.

Harry Truman left Washington on January 20, the day President Eisenhower was inaugurated. At Union Station, he and Mrs. Truman and their daughter, Margaret, were amazed to find a crowd of 5,000 well-wishers singing "Auld Lang Syne." Truman was deeply moved. "I'll never forget this if I live to be a hundred," he said. "And that's just what I expect to do!"

As Truman's train rolled across half the continent to Missouri, similar crowds turned out at every station where he stopped. Even though many of them had voted against the Democratic party, the people seemed to want him to know that it was not a personal rejection. They still liked him.

In Independence, the Trumans received an unforgettable welcome home. A crowd of 10,000 cheered as the train rolled into the depot. The Kansas City American Legion band blasted out the "Missouri Waltz." Around the Truman home on North Delaware Street, another 1,500 neighbors repeated the cheers. Bess was as deeply moved as Harry. She told him the send-off from Washington and this reception in their hometown made the eight frantic years in the White House worthwhile.

Once Harry and Bess got settled in Independence, Truman worked on his memoirs. He turned down numerous offers from corporations to hire him for large amounts of money. One company offered him a half-million dollars. "I could never lend myself to any transaction that would commercialize on the prestige and dignity of the presi-

Home from the political wars, Harry and Bess enjoy their comfortable living room at 219 North Delaware Street in Independence. The house is now open to visitors under the supervision of the National Park Service. (KANSAS CITY STAR)

dency," he said. Fortunately, with the help of his brother, Vivian, and business friends, he was able to sell the old family farm in Grandview for a hefty sum to developers who turned the land into a shopping center. That solved his money worries.

For a while Truman remained active in politics. He did his best to prevent Adlai Stevenson from getting the Democratic nomination in 1956, but could not stop him from running—and losing—again to President Eisenhower. In 1960, he was cool to the candidacy of John F. Kennedy, because he detested his father, Joseph P. Kennedy. But Truman eventually decided that he liked the young man from Boston and campaigned vigorously for him.

After he finished his memoirs, Truman devoted most

The ex-president enjoys a reproduction of his White House Oval Office in the Harry S Truman Library. He visited the library regularly. It is only a few blocks from his home in Independence. (HARRY S TRUMAN LIBRARY)

of his time to building his presidential library, which is only a few blocks from his home in Independence. It contains a replica of his Oval Office, including the sign he always kept on his desk, announcing: "The buck stops here." Another room is devoted to Truman's soldiering years. He persuaded Thomas Hart Benton, the great Missouri painter, to contribute a superb mural and selected most of the other works of art in the building personally.

Truman donated to the library all his presidential papers. But he considered six other rooms in the building just as important as the files containing the millions of pages of documents. These rooms were designed to teach the six functions of the presidency to young people. Exhibits dramatize the president as chief executive, as the chief of state, presiding at various ceremonies, as a legis-

When John F. Kennedy ran for president in 1960, he solicited Truman's support. After some hesitation (because the young senator lacked experience), Truman agreed to back him. When Kennedy won the Democratic nomination, the ex-president campaigned vigorously for him. (HARRY S TRUMAN LIBRARY)

lator, as the leader of his political party, as commander in chief of the army and navy and air force, and as director of the nation's foreign policy.

Another great pleasure in Truman's retirement was his grandchildren. In 1956, his daughter Margaret married newspaperman Clifton Daniel and over the next decade had four sons. Truman frequently came to New York to visit them. He had no hesitation about teaching them some important lessons about life.

One day, the oldest boy, three-year-old Clifton, was riding his hobbyhorse. The horse tipped over and Clifton fell hard. His mother rushed to pick him up and he immediately started to cry. "Leave him alone," Grandfather Truman said.

He pointed to the hobbyhorse. "Pick it up and get back on," he said. Clifton forgot about crying and obeyed orders.

Truman remained intensely interested in the nation's politics. He read several newspapers every day. He also remained a student of history. He often read four books at the same time, switching from one to another when he got bored.

He was dismayed by the way the nation fought the Vietnam War. For Truman, it was another example of Communist aggression, exactly like Korea, and he had no sympathy for those who agitated against the war and urged

In this 1965 photograph, Bess and Harry Truman pose with their three grandsons, from right to left, Clifton, Harrison, and William, their daughter, Margaret, and her husband, Clifton Daniel, who was managing editor of *The New York Times.* Margaret and Clifton later had a fourth son, Thomas. (CLIFTON DANIEL)

the abandonment of South Vietnam. To him, they sounded exactly like Joseph P. Kennedy and the others who had wanted to cut and run from the Chinese Communists.

Truman was particularly dismayed when President Lyndon Johnson decided not to run for reelection in 1968. He compared the situation to 1864, when Abraham Lincoln led a divided nation in the Civil War. "There were politicians and newspapers calling for a premature peace in those days," Truman said. "Lincoln made his election a vote for or against continuing the war. When he won, the south folded up." Truman was convinced that North Vietnam would have done the same thing, if President Johnson had run for reelection and won.

Truman never made any public criticism of President Johnson. He was determined not to become a "croaker" — one of those old men who criticize how the younger generation is running the world. He remained basically optimistic about the future of the United States of America.

In the fall of 1972, Truman became ill and died the day after Christmas at the age of eighty-eight. Only then did historians begin to realize the tremendous achievements of his presidency. Today, with the collapse of communism in Eastern Europe and Russia, and its steady decline in Asia, there is little doubt that he was the architect of victory in the great struggle for the future of the world that began after World War II.

Perhaps the best tribute to Truman was paid by Gen. George Marshall. "The full measure of this man will only be proved by history. But I want to say here and now that there never has been a decision made under this man's administration . . . that has not been made in the best interest of his country. It is not only the courage of these decisions that will live — but the integrity of them."

The years of Truman's life spanned the emergence of

Harry Truman remained a citizen of Independence until his death in 1972 at the age of eighty-eight. He turned down numerous job offers from corporations because he refused to commercialize his presidency. He was proud of his hometown, and his friends and neighbors were equally proud of him. (RLDS CHURCH)

America as a world power. Thanks in large part to him, the United States has used that power to enlarge the freedom of millions of men and women around the globe. One historian has written: "His is the story of an uncommon man whose blessing was that he considered himself a common man."

NOTES ON FURTHER READING

For the most intimate and in many ways the most penetrating look at Harry Truman, his daughter Margaret's biography, *Harry S Truman*, remains the best book. A good companion volume, which has many revealing insights into both parents, is her biography of her mother, *Bess Wallace Truman*.

Alfred Steinberg's *The Man from Missouri* is a solid, reliable study. The same can be said for Jonathan Daniels's *The Man from Independence*. One of the earliest books about Truman, it is still worth reading for its lively anecdotes.

Valuable for its artful combination of pictures and text is Robert H. Ferrell's *Truman: A Centenary Remembrance*. Mr. Ferrell is also the editor of a revealing collection of letters, *Dear Bess,* which Truman wrote to his wife over the years.

Truman wrote a number of books after he left the presidency, including two volumes of memoirs, *Year of Decisions* and *Years of Trial and Hope*. For young readers, probably the best book is *Mr. President*. In the foreword, Truman wrote: "I want the people to understand the presidency as I have experienced it and I want them to know me as I am." This book, full of lively pictures and intimate jottings from diaries and letters, does exactly that.

INDEX

Figures in italics refer to illustrations.

```
--          Fleming, Thomas J.
B                                    15  85
Truman      Harry S Truman,
F              president.
```

DATE			